LOOKING BACK:
THE RUSSIAN REVOLUTION THROUGH THE EYES OF A JEWISH CHILD

ISADORE WEISS

Contributing Authors

Eamon Doherty, PhD
Sylvia Weiss
William "Pat" Schuber
Todd Liebesfeld, Esq.
Joel Liebesfeld
Lewis D. Meixler

authorHOUSE®

AuthorHouse™
1663 Liberty Drive
Bloomington, IN 47403
www.authorhouse.com
Phone: 1-800-839-8640

First published by AuthorHouse 6/26/2009

ISBN: 978-1-4389-8730-9 (sc)
ISBN: 978-1-4490-2717-9 (e)

Printed in the United States of America
Bloomington, Indiana

This book is printed on acid-free paper.

TABLE OF CONTENTS

LIST OF ILLUSTRATIONS

Forward to "Looking Back" by Dr. Eamon P. Doherty

I never met Isadore Weiss personally, but I have interviewed his wife, Sylvia, and his daughter, Deb, heard his audiotapes, and looked at his photo album. I also have an appreciation of the times he lived in from my knowledge of European history, and I read his personal story of his youth in Ukraine during the period of WWI in which he records the difficulties that he and his family faced from poverty, war and the pogroms. Isadore's memoir, written in 1928, only 6 years after coming to the United States, provides a personal insight into the lives of those living in that tumultuous time. Each day was a struggle to survive from his birth in 1908 to his emigration in 1922 from Eastern Europe. As a young child he experienced the troops of Leon Trotsky and the Bolsheviks occupying his home. Simon Petlura and his mercenaries, the Germans and the Polish army also broke into his neighbors' homes and occupied their village. He recalls how each of these unwanted "guests" slept in their beds while they slept on the floor. The "guests" ate their food, which was not plentiful, and many were abusive. People in Isadore's town often had little more than their family and their faith to sustain them. Therefore Isadore's living relatives and I felt it was important to publish this book. His story, "Looking Back" in Part 1 is in his own words and is unedited. The quality of his language, in my opinion, demonstrates Isadore's level of intelligence, observation and education and makes what he says genuine and historic. We are fortunate that Isadore has given us this valuable legacy in the form of a first person memoir. We are also indebted to him for providing his essay, in Part 2 on "What Judaism Means to Me." We thank Sylvia Weiss for her valuable contribution to the book, which provides insight into the life they were able to build together in the United States. Our gratitude also extends to Melvin Weiss, Isadore's nephew, who interviewed Isadore in 1982, and provided the audiotapes of his extensive and well conducted discussions, for this book. We wish to thank Isadore's daughter, Deb Meixler, and her husband Lew for their help in assembling and editing this memoir, and to all the other members of the Weiss family, and to the faculty of Fairleigh Dickenson University for their literary contributions and support. In addition we would like to thank Isadore's grandchildren Michael and Marci Meixler for transcribing the original memoir "Looking Back" into digital format and for creating the website www.isadoreweiss.com where the audio tapes and other material can be accessed. Lastly, but most importantly, we are indebted to Isadore Weiss for creating a wealth of historical material which enabled the creation of this book. So now, because of the enthusiastic support of so many, 80 years after the original memoir was written and 100 years after Isadore's birth, his story is finally published exactly the way he wrote it.

PART 1
LOOKING BACK BY ISADORE WEISS

A STUDENT OF THE
UNIVERSITY OF PITTSBURGH

CHAPTER I
BROTHER'S DEPARTURE TO AMERICA

Dawn had not yet completely routed the darkness of the night. Nevertheless, everyone in our family, including myself- -at that time only five years old- -was already up on this early Sunday morning in the summer of 1912. All of us helped to get Max, the oldest brother, ready to depart to America. Max had just reached his fifteenth year. Father had left instructions before he departed, that at the age of fifteen Max should be sent to join him. Together they would work to earn enough to bring the rest of the family to America.

Three years had now passed since Father had left a wife and six children--five boys and a girl--in this small Russian town. He could not bear to see his children suffer from want of food any longer. He had tried in every way to earn enough money for food at least, but he had been unable to do so. He was not a bad tailor, there were some worse ones in that town; but the customers would come just once, and for some mysterious reason would never cross his threshold again.

Many a night Mother informed us she and father went to bed without supper to save the few crumbs of bread for the children in the morning. Father could not borrow any more, for his debts were already beyond his means to repay. Therefore, after long consultations with Mother, he decided to sell some of the furniture of the house and leave for America, the GOLDEN LAND, as it was popularly known in that part of the world. While in America, he would earn money to pay off his debts and then would bring us over to join him.

To Father's astonishment, however, he did not find GOLD in the streets of America. Instead, he had to take a job for five dollars a week. Here he worked ten and often twelve hours a day. After three years of such labor, he just managed to keep his family abroad supplied with food. There was not enough left to pay any debts. It was, therefore, necessary that Max should join Father to help clear his name and to bring over the rest of the family.

With great interest I watched Max hide his steamship ticket and identification papers. The coach on which he was to leave was often waylaid by robbers, and every one was relieved of all valuables. Max took no chances of losing his precious steamship ticket. He ripped out the lining of his coat; and between the shoulder-pads he placed some of the money, the ticket, and the other papers; he then sewed the coat lining back into place. Everything now was so cleverly hidden that not even a magician could guess what the coat contained.

Just as the sun appeared, Mother told us children to go outside of the town where Max would board the coach. She and Max would follow us. To attract as little attention as possible, we walked in pairs. We did not wish the police to get wind of Max's departure. If the police found it out, he would be held for going to America before serving in the army. It was a great offence to try to cheat the Russian army of a citizen's services. The penalty for this offence might have meant a few years in prison. And so all precautions were taken to keep Max's departure a secret.

Patiently, we awaited the coach's arrival from the town. At last it made its appearance. Each of us kissed Max goodbye, When the coach stopped for Max to board it, Mother, crying, took leave of him. Upon seeing Mother cry, we also burst out in tears. Finally the coachman dragged Max away and drove off. "Don't cry, Mother. Nobody has died that you should cry," I pleaded, associating the crying of an adult only with the death of a person.

"You don't understand, my child. He has to go through a lot of dangers." She went on more to herself than to me, for I could hardly grasp the idea of danger. He is just fifteen, and was never out of town. Now he is to make such a long journey. Worst of all, he is to cross the great, treacherous ocean, where many people drown daily. The majestic word ocean set me to thinking.

Upon reaching the town, I immediately left my mother and sought out my friends, and we started discussing the ocean. We recalled how Jonah was almost eaten by a big fish. Then each one added something of what he had learned from the teacher about the ocean. One comrade, especially, seemed to remember almost everything the teacher had told him about the inhabitants of the ocean:

Large fish, at least the size of a two-story building abounded in the sea. In addition to these monstrous fish, wild, men also were very plentiful there. These wild men had been punished by God and had been assigned to live in the ocean. The huge fish and wild men always tried to capsize the boats plying the ocean. However, they were not always successful. All the boats had sharp knives on the bottoms. The knives were sharp enough to cut the sea creatures in half. But when the knives got dull, the fish and wild men upset the boat and ate the people.

I shuddered to think lest such a fate befall Max. Crying, I ran home and asked Mother whether their stories were true. She told me that the boat Max was aboard would have plenty of sharp knives. The next day, Morris, another brother, ran in out of breath and told us that Max was back under arrest. Upon proper identification by the Mayor, he was given his freedom until the trial. As Max came into the house, we were terribly shocked by his appearance. His clothes were in tatters. His face was all bruised and swollen.

The child in him overwhelmed the man and he burst into tears as he related his experiences at the border: When it got dark, the man, who was to smuggle Brother across the border to Austria, and Max started out from Loskerinin, a Russian town close to the Austrian border. For several hours, they walked through thorny fields. Every once in a while, they imagined that they were being followed, and so ducked close to the ground to avoid being seen. This constant ducking in the thorny bushes caused them great pain because the thorns pierced through their clothes like needles. Upon getting up to continue on their way, the thorns kept tearing away their clothes.

At last they reached a stream about twenty-feet wide. There, the two met a woman with two children. One was four years old and the other was still in the mother's arms. The child seemed to be about two years old. The man who took charge of the woman with the children took the older child on his back. The other child was taken by the man who brought Max. The men cautioned all of them to follow them on foot through the stream without any noise. At about midstream, the water came to their waistlines. It was then that the older boy cried, "Mother, my feet are getting wet."

At that moment, they heard a shout from the guards to return or to be shot down like dogs. As soon as the bank had been reached, the soldiers began beating Brother mercilessly. Not till he had fallen on the ground, half-unconscious, did they stop beating him. Then they ordered him to get up and accompany them. What they did with the woman and children he did not know. When he had wiped his eyes, blinded by tears and blood, she was not there. The soldiers led him back to Loskerinin. From there, he was ordered to be taken home under arrest.

After reciting the above hardships, he vowed that as long as he would live he would not want to go through those sufferings again. It seemed as if they would never cease beating him.

Sunday came around again. Max was now rested and a little more cheerful. Although, when he got back, he vowed that he would not attempt again to cross the border, he now went through the same preparations for his departure as on the preceding Sunday. He had come to the conclusion that it would be better to make another attempt than to rot in the filthy Russian jails.

On the third day our anxieties and fears were allayed. A letter announcing Max's safe arrival in Austria cheered us all. Our hopes were again high. We were certain that before a year passed, Father and Brother would earn enough to pay the debts and bring us to America.

More than a year passed since Max had left us. We, however, were no closer to America than when he left. The combined earnings of Father and Brother did not suffice to do all the things planned. Father now asked that Morris be sent. And in a few weeks, Morris left us, too.

CHAPTER II
AT SCHOOL

It was my second year in the local private school. The boys and girls attending it ranged in age from five to fourteen years. My two older brothers and my sister were also pupils there. They, like the rest, were trying to get an education from the only teacher the school had. My schoolmates several times intimated that our teacher had been a good coach driver in another town before he entered the teaching profession. His brutal beating of the pupils had suggested this idea. He got as much delight out of seeing pupils suffer and writhe under his lash as a coach driver does when he keeps lashing the horses while they have difficulty in getting out of deep mud.

This autumn day the schoolroom was even more dreary than ever. In every corner of the room were pots and pans of all shapes and sizes. In one particular corner a solitary washtub among the smaller vessels, like a giant in the company of pygmies, received the constant dripping from a large leak in the roof. Occasional drippings from smaller holes in the roof found their way into other pots and pans.

The houses in this town had no cellars nor wooden floors. Some of the children in school sat in groups on the earthen floor playing games, talking, and laughing at the top of their voices. Other children ran around the room playing tag. They also were as noisy as children can be, playing an exciting game. Just then I envied all these children. It would take me another hour before I would be able to join in their games. I was only third in line at the teacher's table to recite that day's lesson. The boy reciting had difficulty in making the teacher hear, although he shouted at the top of his voice. The teacher kept on asking him to repeat to make sure that he had read his passage correctly.

At last the boy had finished, and the one next to him took his place at the teacher's side. Another twenty minutes and I would be free for the whole day to play in any manner I pleased, as long as I did not leave the room. Just then the door opened and Mother appeared.

"The rain is still coming down," Mother explained. "I have brought the children their lunch. They may get their feet wet coming home in this torrent. "

The teacher agreed with Mother and ordered me to join my brothers and sister.

"It is my turn next to recite, Mr. Sol," I pleaded. (It was the custom to address everyone in the town by the first name.) "I'll eat when I am through with my lesson."

"You must not make your Mother wait," he shouted. "The afternoon is plenty long enough to give you time for your lesson."

This did not suit me. If I should lose my chance of reciting, I would again have to place myself at the end of the line. This would mean another two or three hours' wait before I would be able to play with the rest of the children who had already recited, and so I decided not to give up so easily. "Mother, wouldn't you wait a few minutes till I get through with my lesson?"

Mother agreed. But the teacher frowned because he could not have his way. In a few minutes he disposed of the pupil before me. I was asked to read only a few lines and was then at liberty to eat lunch.

Mother had just closed the door. The teacher called me over and told me to place myself at the end of the long line.

"But I have already recited," I pleaded.

"Do as I tell you."

Almost on the point of bursting into tears, I took my place as ordered. I now forgot my playmates enjoying themselves without a care. My mind was troubled with thoughts of the punishment I would receive. Would I be disgraced before the class by being put in a corner of the room on my knees? Or would the teacher order me to go around in the schoolroom with my coat inside out for several days? A possible beating with the twenty-thong lash I discounted entirely. This sort of punishment was reserved for boys of ten years or over. I prayed that whatever punishment might come, it should be meted out at once. My friends by their glances pitied me; my enemies seemed to rejoice at my misfortune. The long hours made it unbearable. Now I blushed and got hot all over, thinking of the shame I should have to endure. Then again, the possibility of having to suffer some newly invented punishment made my whole body shiver. On occasions the teacher had been known to invent the most unthought-of punishments.

The room got darker. The kerosene lamp was now lighted. The hour for home going drew near. I began to hope that there would be no punishment. Five pupils were ahead of me. I was certain that the teacher would not find time for me. If only he failed to get to me, he would be sure to forget it all tomorrow.

I was suddenly aroused by the voice of the teacher, "you may now all go and play. You, move over close to me."

Quietly, I watched him open the book to a passage that I never had read before. "Read", he barked.

I made an attempt but stopped too often. The passage was extra hard for me. My mind, on the other hand, could not concentrate on the reading. Instead, I kept wandering off to the thought of what was in store for me next.

Stars suddenly flashed before my *eyes,* and, my left cheek began to smart terribly. As the stars cleared before my eyes, I saw the teacher's open hand advancing to my right cheek. I closed my eyes in time to avoid the flashes, but his second blow pained me even more. I could no longer hold back the tears.

"Read!", he kept on repeating.

Between sobs I read even worse, for I watched his right hand closely to be ready to duck when I would see him raise it. My dodging irritated him even more, and he struck me again and again all over my face. My nose started bleeding. The tears and blood poured down upon the book. Still not content, he took the dreaded lash and applied it on my head, face, and body--wherever he could strike to the best advantage. Writhing under the severe blows, I rolled on the floor. My shrieks and cries might have raised the dead, but they had no effect on him.

After wearing himself out, he put me in a corner. My sobs just would not cease. Even when all my tears had gone dry, my body kept on shaking as in a convulsion. With my sleeves, I tried to wipe the blood, but only smeared it all over my face. The blotches of drying blood drew the skin of my face in all directions. The pain became unendurable.

The clock struck eight. Every pupil eagerly rushed to the cloakroom. This had been a long and trying day for them. Most of them could scarcely endure the sight of the brutal beating, but they could not intervene; it might have meant the same thing for them.

When every one had gone, my brothers put the overcoat over my bloody and dirty clothes. It was a relief to be out of that dingy dungeon. I hoped that I would not have to see it again. I was sure that I had been mistreated. I wondered of what I was guilty, to have been punished so severely. Not even once had the teacher mentioned the reason for acting as he did. It seemed that he had given that beating because I could not read the passage well. To me it all seemed unfair. I determined not to step into that classroom again.

My mother did not agree with me. She tried to make me see the good of an education. And there were no other schools in town. I failed to see the good of an education accompanied by such brutalities. The next morning, however, all washed and clothed in a clean suit, I was sent to school.

CHAPTER III
THE NIGHT BEFORE THE STORM

One evening a celebrated singer was to give a concert-- a rare occurrence in our town. Only second-rate singers ever visited us.

All day long I planned how I might gain admittance to the concert hall, for a ticket was out of the question. I had no money and Mother could not spare any, for I well knew that there was just enough for food and clothing from what Father sent from America. Besides, Mother had great difficulty in paying for our schooling. The teacher had threatened several times, within my hearing, to send us all home if she did not pay our tuition regularly. I, therefore, decided that the best way for me to get into the big synagogue where the concert was to be held was to steal in unnoticed, if that were possible.

An hour before the concert the whole town was in a hub-bub. All flocked toward the synagogue. Those that could not buy tickets came to get at least a glimpse at the important personage. Those who were fortunate enough to have tickets stood in two long lines, extending from the doors of the synagogue through the large hall and into the street two blocks away. Each one was eager to get inside to his seat. Everyone who held a ticket feared that too many tickets had been sold, and that meant that unless he got in early, he might not get in at all; and so there was much pushing and shoving in the lines. Every once in a while a big fellow came along and tried to force his way into the middle of a line, but the people were packed too closely for anyone to break through. With an oath the bully would then take his rightful place at the end of the line like any other person.

I took my place in the line although I had no ticket. The day was hot. Great beads of perspiration rolled down my cheeks. I found no time to wipe them away, for I was constantly on the lookout in order not to be shoved out of my place. I also, being small, tried to keep the pressure of the crowd from smothering me. Every time there was the least little change in the line in front of me, the people behind me surged forward as if a ten- foot space had been made. I hoped in this way to be thrust finally into the concert hall. I could see from where I was standing that the men at the door were having difficulty in collecting the tickets. Once through the door, I felt that I would be safe.

Near the entrance the line seemed to move faster. My small body was wedged in between two tall men. Before I realized it, I was inside the large synagogue.

This synagogue was one of the show places of our town. When a person of any consequence visited the village, it was always pointed out to him. Many legends were woven around it. The old men said that only two other synagogues like it existed in the world. The same artist had decorated all three, but the decorations in the third place of worship had not been finished. While the artist was painting the high domelike ceiling, he lost his equilibrium and fell to his death. That synagogue, wherever it was, had remained as the dead artist had left it.

Our synagogue was a large square hall. Twenty huge columns supported the high, heavy dome. These columns had not been put in when the place had originally been built. They had been added much later. A story surrounded the reconditioning of the place. The contractor who had undertaken to repair the synagogue had set a definite date on which the work was to be completed. In order to fulfill his contract, the man had rushed his work; and to the astonishment of every one, he had his men work at it on the first Sabbath. The protest of the town had no effect on him. He maintained, since the agreement did not call for a stoppage of work on that day (a clause, which the Elders of the synagogue had never dreamed of putting in, because they did not imagine that anyone would dare work on the Sabbath, (especially on a job like this), then he would work when he pleased. The next day, the story went on, the man died. Every one said that God had punished him for his rashness.

On the walls of the synagogue, in places where persons had rubbed accidentally, reading matter could be seen. Upon approaching closer, one could see on the walls beautiful lettering overlaid with a thick layer of dust and cobwebs. It was said that the contents of the Old Testament were to be found on these walls. This could never be verified, however, for dust had covered the walls for decades. To wipe them off was considered sacrilegious. Because the walls had not been cleaned during the first year of the building's existence, they were doomed never to be cleaned. Such was the custom, and no one would dare break it. It was fortunate that the floor had been cleaned during the first year; otherwise, we would have had to walk in dust up to our ankles or worse.

Turning to the high domelike ceiling, one could make out a picture quite different from those on the walls, though also overlaid with dust and grime. In a background once rich and colorful in which red and gold predominated, different wild animals seemed to have chosen this holy dome for their abode. All were lifelike because the artist had painted them in their natural colors. Lions and tigers roamed freely, foxes also prowled about, and elephants with big tusks completed the picture. Nor were snakes wanting. They could be seen winding themselves around the limbs of the trees. This picture gave many of us our only chance to get acquainted with the various animals of the world, for our town had no zoo, and circuses never stopped.

Rough benches, arranged in orderly rows, furnished the seats. At first I thought of taking a seat. But I soon perceived that people who did not have tickets were forcibly ejected, if found in seats. Since there was no standing room, I decided to crawl under a bench and thus listen to the concert.

The position was not very comfortable. I had to lie on one side, since I desired to face the singer. Soon I grew tired, the excitement of getting into the hall had now worn off; and, before the concert started, I fell asleep.

I had just awakened. The place was in complete darkness. I tried to figure out where I was. I realized that my resting place was very different from the feather bed at home. I felt it with my hand. It was the hard floor. Had I fallen out of bed during my sleep? I tried to raise myself up to get back into bed. Something was in my way over my head. Cautiously, I felt in front of me, back of me; there was no obstruction. I raised my hand to make out what the object above me might be. Slowly, I felt it from side to side. Being wider-awake by this time, I made out that the thing over me was a bench.

I now recalled how I had worked my way into the hall. It suddenly dawned upon me that I was alone in the synagogue at this late hour. I recollected the stories told about ghosts and spirits frequenting this place in the darkness of the night. A cold sweat covered me at the thought. Trembling, I slowly raised my eyes to the altar. I tried to cover them with my hand, but my hand lay coldly by my side--I could not move it. Covered from head to feet, figures in white robes surrounded the altar. To and fro they swayed. This spectacle, like a magnet, drew my glance.

All my faculties forsook me at this sight. I tried to get up. I could not. I tried to scream. Then darkness!

****

When I opened my eyes, I was in bed. Beside me sat Mother with a worried look on her face. I recollected the white-cloaked spirits and shuddered. There before me they still kept swaying at the altar. Had it been merely a dream or could it have been true? Mother avoided answering these questions; so did the rest of the family.

Later in the day, I questioned Mother again. I told her that the visions kept coming back to me. An explanation, I thought, might give me rest. With some hesitation, Mother began:

The night before when my bedtime came, I was missed. Mother, however, was not troubled much by this. She thought that I might be around the synagogue, and when the concert was over, I would come home.

About eleven o'clock, when everybody had come home from the concert, I had not made my appearance. Mother decided to wait another half hour before looking for me. Still I did not come. Mother then made the rounds of my friends; woke them up to find out if they had seen me during the early hours of the night. No, none of them had seen me.

Frightened, Mother ran to the police to report my disappearance. Together they rushed to the ticket collectors and ushers who had been employed at the concert. They said it was impossible for me to have been in the hall. If I had been overlooked by the ticket takers, I would surely have been discovered by the ushers. Then I would have been ejected from the place, because there was no standing room, and seats were occupied only by ticket holders. This information caused them to search for me elsewhere than in the synagogue.

Meanwhile searching parties had been formed and they looked for me all over the town, with no success. One group of men was bold enough to approach the synagogue at this late hour. After midnight no one passed near the synagogue. If a person had to go to a place that could be reached more quickly by taking the street past the synagogue, the person would avoid this short cut for a more circuitous way. They looked about the place, but did not see me.

Then horror of horrors! They heard unearthly screams. They were frozen to the spot. The cries were repeated. No one ever heard of spirits screaming. It was true that romantic boys and girls who stayed out late at night had reported that sometimes while passing the synagogue in a group, they had heard praying in loud voices. But no one had ever reported such unearthly noises as these.

A few of the men summoned up courage and with a lighted candle cautiously walked into the synagogue to investigate. Upon opening the doors, they were surprised to find nothing unusual in the place. They were terribly frightened, however, and did not look right in front of them. One suggested that the spirits might be hiding under the benches. But the rest decided to investigate. Taking a few steps forward, the leading man stumbled over something. Seeing this the others fled. He, too, was about to turn and rush out; reason, however, urged him to examine the obstacle at his feet. The candlelight fell on a small unconscious figure.

Immediately he rushed out with me in his arms. He bade two men to run for a doctor. It took the doctor a quarter of an hour to restore me to consciousness.

The same day, I learned that news had just reached MINKOVITZ, this far-off South Russian town, that war with Germany had been declared.

Chapter IV
WAR WONDERS

On August 2, mobilization was in full swing. Countless men passed by from nearby towns and villages to Nova Ushitza, the county seat, about ten miles distant from our town. There they were to register and be examined. All young men, twenty-one to thirty years of age if in good health, were enlisted immediately. Those who had military service were sent to the front; the others were sent to training camps.

The men were not anxious to leave their homes. Many had to leave families, wives and children; others, their parents, brothers, and sisters. The harvesting time was close, too. If there were not enough people to gather the crops, it might mean starvation to many.

In the market place there were always several groups of men discussing the war. In whispers they expressed their opinions. They did not see why there should be a war. If Russia quarreled with Germany, why should they go and be killed? What had Russia done for them to demand their lives? Even now they were little better than serfs. Many times they had been beaten by the nobles, whose lands they tilled. They had no choice, however. To the war they must go or they might go--to Siberia!

****

Before the war had lasted a year, more men were drafted. This time the ages were between eighteen and forty- five. The doctors at Nova Ushitza did not scrutinize the men very closely now. If a man had good eyes, was not hard of hearing, and had no other very serious handicap, he was good enough to be a soldier. After this second draft, the town contained only old men, women, children, and those who were absolutely unfit for military service.

****

Meanwhile the war had its advantages, too. Before the war, we had occasionally heard people tell of a "horseless carriage." But we could scarcely believe that such a thing existed.

One day we heard that the "horseless carriage" had come to town. The whole town rushed to the market place to see this wonder. The teacher, who also wanted to see the strange vehicle, dismissed us from school. We lost no time in getting there. Excitedly, I pushed through the crowd to observe it closely. We wondered at its shining body. We touched its pneumatic rubber tires and remarked that it must be very comfortable to ride in it. Then our attention was caught by a shining nickel face on the right side of the windshield. It was a funny looking face, with its mouth wide open, and with shining, even teeth glistening from it. We wondered what this distorted face's use could be. Someone suggested that this face gave the power to the car.

At last the officials of the "horseless carriage" entered it. Closely we watched one of them crank the motor. He got into the vehicle but it could not move on account of the crowd about it. Politely, they asked us to step aside so that they might leave. We, however, did not want this wonder to leave our midst so quickly, and accordingly we did not move from our places. The soldiers were in a dilemma. They did not want to start the car for fear of killing or maiming someone.

Impatient, they began to curse and to talk loudly to us, but it was of no avail.

A strange and weird sound pierced our ears! Terror- stricken, we took a look at the wide-open mouth of the shining distorted face, whence the sound issued, and fled for our lives in all directions. It was an uncanny sound! So strange to the ears! We never had heard anything like it. At a safe distance, we turned and looked back; the car was now roaring on its way.

Daily, automobiles went roaring through the town. Many times the local horses seeing these strange things rush by would get frightened and rush wildly around town. The coaches or wagons drawn by these maddened horses were often wrecked.

****

Quite a few motorcycles rushed by. At first not one of them stopped. Every time that one went by, the whole town rushed out to view it speeding on its way. We speculated as to its purpose. One man said that he observed that each motorcycle driver carried a leather bag at his side. These bags, he said, contained secret notes. Therefore, according to his theory, these drivers, who were in a great hurry to deliver them, never stopped. He further suggested that we call these things on two wheels "Gossip-Carriers." From then on, this was our town's official name for a motorcycle. It was better than not having any name for it.

Once a "Gossip-Carrier" stopped to deliver a message to the Mayor. Everyone examined the machine. The man did not stay long. However, as soon as he delivered the message, he mounted again and asked a few of the older boys to push him a little way on it. Several boys gladly volunteered. When they pushed the two-wheel machine for about a block, it started and sped away. The boys got the greatest thrill out of this experience. They never failed to remind the rest that they had helped to start a "Gossip-Carrier." Here was something that they would be able to tell their grand-children.

****

One day a dull roar was heard over our heads. We could not remove our eyes from the majestic spectacle'. Not until the airplane was lost to our sight did we start discussing it. This was a mystery altogether beyond us. We could not understand the automobile, but yet it moved on the solid ground. It was truly a miracle to see something sail along in the air.

One cold winter day there was a report that an airplane had arrived two miles outside the town. This news traveled fast. In less than a half hour, scores of people left town to see it.

On the ground the deep white snow glistened in the shining sun. Nevertheless, nearly the whole town, wrapped securely to keep out the cold, trudged along in the deep frozen snow. The creaking of shoes in the snow was pleasing to the ear, and every one enjoyed the two-mile walk, although it was extremely cold.

At last we drew near the thing standing on two wheels, with its tail resting on the snow. On each side, a huge wing was extended. The body had two cockpits. We were surprised to see two common, ordinary men standing beside the plane. The men were very civil. They told us that they were out of gas. No damage had been done to the plane in this forced landing. A few minor repairs were needed to put the plane in shape again. To the best of their ability, they explained to us how an airplane flies, and ended with an invitation to come and see them off when the snow melted.

****

That same winter the Germans made constant attacks on our army. They kept coming closer and closer to the Ukraine. The seriously wounded passed daily through our town on wagons. They presented a terrible sight. Some men had their heads and faces so bandaged that only their mouths, noses, and eyes were visible. Many were legless; still others were without hands, or had one hand, all the fingers of which were missing. We shuddered to think what misery these men would have to go through, if an early death did not claim them.

These were not the only poor wretches that we saw. The first group of German prisoners that passed through our town presented a spectacle even worse--about a thousand miserable wretches, hatless, bootless, and in rags. Through the deep snow that sometimes lay on the ground. For a month or longer, these unhappy men trudged into town. They must have been made of iron to have been able to endure the extreme cold so scantily clad. Not one of them was clothed sufficiently to keep out the biting cold. Those that had rags on their feet were no better off than those that went barefoot. The long march had worn their rags out and the snow slid in through the holes and tortured them even worse. No energy was left in any of them. Some of them cried. Some just stood with their heads bowed, looking at the snow. How the guards could endure to see such misery for hours was beyond us. The guards' hearts must have been made of stone. The prisoner's limbs must have been completely numbed with the cold. They were beyond the stage of feeling the cold now, however. They felt something worse. Spears seemed to be piercing their bodies. Their faces were distorted from pain.

Upon questioning the guards, it was disclosed that these wretches had a half-pound of dry bread each for the whole day. The next day, they would receive the same size ration. It was also learned that they would spend the night outside in this extreme cold.

The leading citizens of the town asked the guards to allow the town to feed the prisoners and quarter them. No, the guards refused to give permission. They had orders, they said, to treat them so and they would not disobey.

We thought that if the guards saw us actually bringing food, they would not stop us from distributing it. In a short time enough food was donated by each family to appease the prisoners' hunger at least for the night. Some brought clothing to give to the most ragged of the group.

To our surprise, we were forbidden to distribute the food. The cruel, well-fed guards would not allow us to approach closer than two feet.

The prisoners' faces brightened up at the sight of the baskets of food. In a strange tongue they clamored for it. Those that were composed and quiet when we first saw them now broke down in sobs and with the rest waved their hands, shouted, and made gestures to indicate that they were hungry.

We could no longer endure the sight. We took the food and clothing and threw them into their midst. Poor devils, they fell on the ground and fought each other for a piece of bread. The few pieces of clothing that had been thrown into their midst were torn into shreds. One seized one part of a garment and another took hold of the other part, and, in their eagerness to gain possession, tore it. Each then looked at his half and simultaneously burst out in a hideous, maddening laugh. Then, they threw themselves again on the ground to obtain some food at least.

Some laughed out loud as they got hold of a loaf of bread. Others cried, their tears falling on the hard loaves, making them softer after they had been trodden upon and trampled in the dirty snow.

I could bear it no longer. "Mother," I cried," what did they do to be treated so."

Mother grabbed me by the hand and drew me away.

"Hush, lest anybody hear you. Don't ask such questions anymore."

The whole night, I had no rest. Their painful faces reappeared. The fight for food was again reenacted. Oh! It was horrible. I buried my face in my pillow and cried myself to sleep.

The following morning, the whole town felt relieved, for the horde of wretched, suffering, starving Germans had passed on.

CHAPTER V
INDEPENDENCE

Towards the spring of 1917, the front kept coming closer to our town. At night, rumblings of far-off cannon were heard. We were not certain, however, how far away from our town the fighting was. Some said it was twenty miles distant, others fifty. We lived in constant fear lest the enemy enter our town. We did not expect mercy from them. It was reported that they were unusually cruel, that they robbed and beat the people, and burned their houses, and pillaged their fields. Wherever they passed, it was said that they left the place desolated.

The repeated cannonading was now not only heard during the stillness of the night, but also during the day. One day the rumblings seemed unusually loud and near; the next day they receded and seemed farther away.

The few days that these rumblings were heard, everybody was in terror. We stayed within doors and were afraid to go out upon the streets. We took inventory of the few cellars in the town, for only wine merchants had cellars. We tried to fix in our minds the cellar nearest to our house. In case the fighting reached the town, we wanted to be sure of the cellar to which we would flee for refuge.

Since the booming of cannon continued for several days, we got used to it. Little by little the town began to go about its business. We found, that when we were busy the strain was not so great. We expected to hear these rumblings daily; in fact, we desired to hear them. For, by their sound, we could tell how close the enemy was. If the cannonading happened to cease for an hour, we began to fear again for we were uncertain whether the enemy were advancing or retreating.

Meanwhile, a detachment of soldiers had reached town. Without wasting much time, it took possession of one of the four hills surrounding the town. Our town lay in a valley surrounded by four towering hills. From any of these hills the whole town could be seen, also what was taking place on the other three hills. The soldiers occupied the hill that faced the one on which the Germans would make their appearance, if they reached the town.

As soon as the detachment had arrived at the hill, they started digging trenches. Day and night they worked at them. We would seek out a place in town where it was easy for us to see the soldiers digging on the hilltop. We were both amused and frightened by these preparations. Trench digging was new to us, and with great interest we watched them. At the same time, we were secretly alarmed, for we felt that these preparations were ominous of some disaster to come upon us.

Early in May, news reached town that the Czar had been dethroned. At first we could not believe it. Who, we asked ourselves, had the courage to raise his hand against such an awe-inspiring personage? Strange as it seemed, it appeared to be true. For the person who brought this news to the town was not molested by the police. Formerly such reports were branded as treasonable and meant banishment to Siberia. Not even behind locked doors would a person have said anything against the Czar. The dreaded secret police always had a way of finding out things.

Within a few days, the people learned about the arrest of the Czar and his family. Everyone was wild with joy. Peasants flocked to the town. Daily orators talked of freedom. With their flowery words they incited the populace. Every one shouted, 'DALLOI NICKOLAI - DOWN WITH NICHOLAS'. They cried themselves hoarse repeating these two words. Then someone with a club attacked the statue of the Czar, which stood in the public square. In a short time, hundreds of fists were pounding against it. Then from out of nowhere appeared crowbars and heavy iron hammers. The crowd became furious when the statue resisted their repeated attacks. Someone at last succeeded in beheading the likeness of the Czar. With the rage of maniacs the mob seized the head, spat upon it, and then threw it on the ground where it was trodden upon and rolled about. At last it was broken into fragments under the constant beating of the iron hammers. Not until the statue was completely demolished did they leave it. Other statues of notables found a similar fate. By nightfall not a single statue remained in town.

Having done away with the likenesses of the nobility, the mob still was not content. The following day, the villagers returned and attacked the nobles themselves who for hundreds of years had made the people suffer. They broke into the palatial houses, and those unhappy nobles who had not had the foresight to flee, were attacked and brutally treated. They were literally torn limb for limb by the enraged mob. Then followed wholesale pillaging. Every peasant grabbed what he could. One carried away a phonograph; another silver plate, others seized fine clothing and luxurious rugs. The costly furniture was broken, and finally the houses were set on fire. That night fires raged in all parts of the town. The people never tried to put them out. Simon, the wood- chopper, was now the proud owner of a phonograph. He and his family did not enjoy the music of this rare instrument alone. They were very kind. Everyone was allowed to come to listen to it. Those that came first found seats in the small house. The rest stood around outside, leisurely listening to the marvelous music box. Now, the people did not fear that they would be driven away from the windows or their tasks. Their taskmasters were either dead or fugitives. They, the people, might do as they pleased.

****

Late in May handbills were passed around. These bills announced a big parade in Nova Ushitza, the county seat, on the last day of the month. My Uncle immediately hired a wagon and a team of horses for that day. We were surprised to have Uncle do such a thing. We wondered where he would get the money to pay for it, since he did not make enough to feed his family.

****

Early in the morning of May 31, Uncle woke my two brothers, my sister, and me. We got into the wagon and proceeded to the market place. There Uncle stopped and sold seats to eager people wanting to see the big spectacle. Three persons were enough to pay for the wagon and horses. Then we started out. On the road, we passed hundreds of people walking to Nova Ushitza. Men, women, and children of all ages were directing their steps to the county seat.

On the outskirts of the town we met people gaily dressed in their holiday clothes. They were all enthusiastic and joyous. Each one seemed to have forgotten that a war was still being fought and not far off at that.

The town was filled with people. The women had their hair gathered up with red ribbons. The men wore red ribbons pinned on their breasts. We were told also to provide ourselves with like ribbons if we wished to mix in the crowd.

At every house waved a bright red flag. A festive spirit was in the air. Everybody was expectant.

About ten o'clock in the morning we heard music approaching the market place. Before long we saw an orderly parade at the head of which was a big brass band. All kinds of banners were carried by important-looking individuals. Red flags were carried by almost everybody in the procession. Slowly the crowd made its way to a big lawn surrounding a church. In front of the church, a high platform decorated with red flags had been erected. As the parade came to the platform, several people mounted it and seated themselves on chairs. Then through the long hours of the day, while we sweltered in the hot sun, speeches were made by the individuals on the rostrum. They talked about the sufferings of the people under the old regime, and they painted a UTOPIA under the new one. Each orator stressed the fact that the land would be divided, and no person would be in need. The mob kept applauding in loud hurrahs. And as each individual finished his speech, the people boisterously broke into the strains of the MARSEILLAISE: Stavoi Rabotchi Naro'd!. Wake up 0'Ye Laboring Class!

Towards night clouds appeared in the sky. Without much warning rain came down. The speakers did not cease talking. Out of respect for them we, too, stood our ground in that heavy torrent. The flags, which had been dyed, faded in our hands. We did not dare lower them, however. Finally, the celebration was over. Dripping wet, we scrambled into the wagon and hurried home.

Chapter VI
A Pogrom

The enthusiasm arising out of the revolution apparently strengthened the morale of our forces at the front. Although the fighting seemed close to our town in the early spring, our army succeeded in blocking the Germans. Thus the two armies kept fighting without much advantage to either side. Through the whole summer the now familiar cannonading continued, but nothing more happened.

In September 1917, there were rumors that our army could not withstand the constant onslaughts of the Germans any longer. We were told that the Russians in their retreat were holding pogroms, murdering, pillaging and robbing the Jewish inhabitants of the towns through which they passed. They attacked the Jewish women and burned their homes. The ignorant peasants who now could no longer pillage and murder the nobles, for there was not one of them left, joined the soldiers in these heinous brutalities.

For several days the whole Jewish populace in our town lived in doubt and fear. We could not realize that our own countrymen could be guilty of such acts. Yet we feared this might be true, we could still recollect the attacks on the nobles. Whenever a mob is led by an unscrupulous leader, it follows its emotions and does not stop to reason. At least, there was some justification for their treatment of the nobles. Long years of suffering had stored up enough hatred in them not to have any scruples in making these monsters suffer. But what grievance had they against the Jews? We had never enslaved these peasants; we had never tortured them. In many cases, we were treated by the nobles very much in the same way as the peasants. A noble would flog a Jew with as little scruple as he would a peasant. He would insult him; call him, "A dog of a Jew," and many other such degrading epithets. We could not make any complaints, for these same nobles were the officials and judges of the district. Thus, just like the peasants, we had to suffer and keep quiet. Naturally we sympathized with the peasants, for our treatment made us feel as if we were akin. Now it was reported that the peasants had turned against us. Instead of helping us to repel those brutal soldiers, they had joined them. It was incredible!

Nevertheless, no matter how false these reports might have seemed, our town believed in preparation. Secretly, under the leadership of a Jewish young man and a friendly Christian youth, the Jewish young men, some two hundred of them, organized into a sort of militia. The two leaders, who were home on leave from the army, somehow procured rifles and ammunition. These they handed out to the secret militia. Daily the militia was assembled and instructed in the use of firearms.

The two youthful leaders thought of everything. At night the militia took turns in patrolling the streets. The rest of the militia slept in their clothing, ready to rush to the protection of the town at the call of the patrol. The call agreed upon was to be two blasts of a horn.

It was a day late in September. The sun's rays had colored the leaves into many shades. That day there was a heavy stillness in the air. We sensed this depressing stillness even at school. The teacher was less harsh. He allowed every child to play and called for no recitations that day. A few shots were heard. The teacher immediately dismissed school and told everyone to run home.

My brother and I, who were then the only ones in our family attending school, were frightened and ran into the street. Already the storekeepers had locked their stores. We could see the people closing their shutters and bolting their doors. The repeated shots we had heard came from the market place where the soldiers had set up two machine guns. They kept grinding away at them. Meanwhile the militia had scattered themselves in different parts of the town. They piled themselves in narrow alleys and shot into the air, hoping in this way to frighten the robbers: These few hundred youths did not dare offer open opposition, for the machine guns would mow them down in no time. So they had to be content with the warfare in the hidden alleys.

We kept running from one group of the militia to another. At each group of youths we stopped for protection, and then rushed off to another safety zone, thus getting close to our destination. Meanwhile, we could see on the hills neighboring peasants with sacks coming down upon the town. Some rode in wagons, hoping to fill them with the spoils.

At last we reached our grandfather's house, which happened to be nearer the school. We beat on the door for several seconds without getting a reply. We were frantic. We knocked again and cried to those within, telling them who we were. Finally the door was opened a little and we were dragged in more dead than alive. There we found Mother, Brother and Sister, who had preceded us. Mother did not feel safe to remain at home with the two young children. Then she explained why Grandpa did not open the door so quickly. He thought soldiers wanted access. But when they recognized our cries they were relieved and let us in.

Presently we saw through a corner of the window two soldiers enter the street. They apparently had gotten by the watchful militia. We were horrified at this thought. That meant of course that they had slaughtered the innocent youths. We could explain it no other way, for we believed that the entrance of each street was guarded by militia.

On one porch an old insane woman sat basking herself in the sun. She was unaware of what was going on in the town. The two scoundrels walked over to her. They began to talk to her, but she did not reply. Both of them started beating her with their long lashes.

My seventy-year old grandfather could not bear to see this act of cruelty. In spite of our efforts to stop him, he rushed over to the unhappy woman and reprimanded the brutes for doing such a cowardly thing. Laughing boisterously, the two devils turned upon him. Mercilessly, they lashed him until he fell down, apparently unconscious. Then they kicked him and rolled him on the ground for amusement. They then turned once more upon the poor woman. Now without interference, they finished the woman in the same manner as they had Grandpa.

They wanted something else. They knocked on a few doors, but got no answer. They tried to break one in, without success, however. They raged, "Damn Jews, open your doors,"

"Look," shouted one of the hounds, "there, through the opening in the shutter, peers a girl." Enraged that he could not lay his dirty hands on the innocent girl, he coolly drew his revolver and shot at her.

The two soldiers had departed but no one dared to help Grandpa and the old woman. We feared lest other soldiers might come into the street. Thus we sat behind bolted doors in anguish and fear. It was maddening to see these cowardly deeds, and still more so to listen to the quick rat-ta-tat of the machine guns, which continued for an hour. In constant fear we cowered in the houses--women, children, old men. All the young men were on the streets, shooting it out with an army.

The machineguns finally stopped and the scattered shots of the militia also ceased. The utter stillness was beyond endurance. No one dared to leave a house to find out the reason for the stillness. Had the militia been slain? Will our town be the next to be attacked and its inhabitants slain in cold blood? These thoughts drove us nearly mad.

For half an hour we were tortured thus. Finally, we saw some of our young men, perspiring and exhausted from their recent ordeal, rush into the street. They asked everyone to come out of the houses and they told us of the valor of their two leaders.

The two young men had seen that the militia's ammunition was getting low and realized that as soon as the firing would cease the soldiers would start their bloody work. They decided not to incur such a risk. Instead each made bold to approach the two machine gunmen. Luck favored them and each leader succeeded in shooting down a machine gunner. The rest of the soldiers of the army were terrified by the valor of the two men and fled, abandoning the two dead men and the machine guns. The peasants from the neighboring villages also left the town.

The news was heartening but our fears were not allayed very much. Just recently we had witnessed what one division of an army had done. What would the rest of the army, in full retreat, do? Would our few hundred young men be able to rout the whole army?

With these sad thoughts torturing us, we administered aid to my grandfather and the old woman. They soon regained consciousness. We then tried to discover any other casualties. The girl, who had been shot at by the enraged soldier, we found to have been wounded slightly in the arm. A woman, whose husband was in America, together with her fourteen year old daughter, had been attacked by several of the soldiers in their homes. Overwhelmed with shame and grief they tried to commit suicide by cutting their throats, but some of the neighbors arrived in time to prevent them. Our house, which was also on the outskirts of the town, was broken into and sacked. The few clothes that we had were taken. The pillows were torn open and the whole house was full of feathers.

Night approached. We feared the horrors that the night might bring. Every house was heavily bolted. Not a light was to be seen. Outside the Militia was on constant guard but what could they do to prevent an army from carrying out their intentions. They were already weary from the experiences of the day. None of them beside the leaders ever had served in the army; they were not used to this nerve-racking business. Most of them were still very young-boys in fact. All of the able bodied young men had gone to the front to fight for the Fatherland. Only the young and the unfit were left. Those serving in the Militia were between the ages of fourteen and eighteen.

Five thousand souls locked in for safety prayed that no harm might come to their children or their brothers outside. Every house was a house of prayer. Subdued sobs and cries mingled with the prayers, which must have gone straight up to Heaven. Hot tears rolled down everybody's cheeks. We did not think of food or drink. Our thoughts were bent on the safety of our beloved ones, both here and at the front.

We shuddered to think that we had to fight our own countrymen for our very existence. What had we, innocent old men, women, and children done, that our own Russian army should try to avenge its retreat on us Jews? Were we not as human as they? Were not our women as honorable as theirs? Were not our men giving their lives for their Fatherland? What could we now expect from the enemy after being treated so cruelly by our own army?

Such were the thoughts that ran through every one's mind. Oh that the day would only dawn. Darkness is so uncertain. It only added to the already existing grief and fear. We felt as if the devil himself were lurking in every room. Huddled together, we sat with our backs to the wall of an inner room for we imagined ourselves being stabbed in the back.

The dawn approached. The old men crept cautiously into the streets. They returned with the report that everything was quiet.

This good news dispelled our fears of the night. One by one we went out into the streets. Groups gathered in the market place and discussed the happenings of the previous day. For a while we seemed to forget the danger that still hovered over us, with the passing of the rest of the army.

Two soldiers on horses galloped into town. They came so suddenly and unexpectedly that we found no time to flee to our homes. They approached a group of bystanders and asked for the leaders of the militia. Seeing that every one hesitated to answer them, they added that they wanted to ask for permission to pass through the town.

At this explanation, we gaped at them in astonishment and still hesitated. We were surprised that a whole army would ask permission of a few hundred youths to allow it to pass without molestation. Our men would be only too glad to leave them alone if they would not bother us. We feared that this request was a mere camouflage. What if they seized our leaders and killed them!

There was no escape, however. The two brave young men were accordingly informed and they fearlessly walked over to the soldiers. The latter repeated their request and added that the peasants of the surrounding villages enjoined them not to pass our town without permission from the Jews. The peasants related that they were in town the previous day and saw how the Jews mowed down a division of the army with machine guns and cannon. The army therefore decided not to take any chances.

The permission was gladly given. For the next four days, our army kept passing constantly through our town. Much to our surprise, they did not molest us in the least. On the fifth day, the Germans were in possession of the town.

Chapter VII
THE GERMANS

The Germans entry into our town impressed us very much. In clean, dull green uniforms thousands of Germans marched into town. At the head of this column marched a large band playing the most beautiful strains. It was more like a parade. As we heard the music, we children ran towards it. By this time the Germans had stopped in the market place. The band, however, formed into a semi-circle and kept playing at the direction of a man, who kept shaking his hands, in one of which was a small stick. This all seemed strange to us. We wondered why the man kept shaking his hands. All the Russian bands we had heard and seen played without having a man in front of them shaking his hands at them. We were also fascinated by the extra large bass-horns. We admired the very large drum drawn by a pony on a two- wheeled carriage.

This all seemed to draw us to the Germans. We forgot that they were our enemies. We crowded around them and were not rebuked. On the contrary, they amused themselves with us. They smiled at us and we drew still closer. They patted our heads, pinched our cheeks, and were very friendly. At any minute we expected to be eaten alive by them, but much to our surprise it never happened.

After the band had played for half an hour, it stopped. Then the officers started going around town quartering the Germans. Three soldiers were put in each house. We got our share.

At first, we feared them somewhat. We had heard so much about their cruelty; it seemed impossible that all of the reports were false. When we started thinking that these same men were, just a few days ago, killing our own men in battle, we could not help feeling terrorized in their presence. The difference in their language also helped to heighten our fears of them. We were not entirely at ease when the three sat at night and talked among themselves. What if they were planning to murder us in our beds!

Contrary to our expectations, the quartered troops did not leave the town in the morning. Instead, others passed by without stopping. Heavy artillery rumbled by on the cobbled highway, cavalry and infantry also passed in great numbers. Then followed what looked to be unimportant officers in many beautiful automobiles.

This procession lasted for a whole day. Then all became quiet, and the troops that entered the town first settled down for a good rest.

Before a month had passed, the town was in order. Business was transacted in the same peaceful manner as before the war. The Germans tried to teach us to be sanitary. Everyone was forced to sweep clean the sidewalk in front of his house. All were prohibited from dumping waste in the gutters. Everyone was compelled to dump garbage in a can and other refuse in huge boxes built into the ground in every street. These cases were emptied during the night monthly.

As a result of this, the town started to present a better appearance. It felt good to walk around on clean sidewalks. It felt much better not to have to fear lest some waste be dumped on you from an upper floor. This better sanitation decreased the amount of sickness and death. Furthermore, the army doctor, attended without pay, the sick of the town as well as the sick soldiers.

Little by little we got to understand each other. The three soldiers quartered in our house saw our plight. They grew to realize that we could not get any help from America because of the bloody war. These three rough orderlies took pity on us and daily brought us bread, potatoes, and other vegetables to feed the family. We were only sorry that we could not express outright our gratitude in words. Soon the winter came and Mother began to worry about the heating of the house. We had no wood stored away, and. we had no money to buy any. The Germans again came to our rescue. Every morning the three kind men would come home with firewood to last for a week. Then they would return to their kitchen and bring us the food. They themselves heated the stoves and they spared no wood. That winter we enjoyed a warmer house than we ever had before.

At nights the three friendly Germans would gather us children around them and tell us stories in their strange language. We could follow them by watching their lighted- up, enthusiastic faces. After the stories they would make playthings for us. They were experts with a penknife and an ordinary piece of wood. They shaped all kinds of playthings out of this wood making soldiers with rifles, cavalry men, cannons, and countless other things.

As the signs of Spring appeared, they began to prepare to leave the town. Early in April the troops left our town. Everyone in town was grieved. We did not mind so much their advance farther into our country. By now we had no love for our Fatherland. We could not have after having been treated so by our soldiers. We were grieved to see these fine men, who had showed us how to live clean, brought order from chaos, heated our houses, and fed us, go to their deaths. They had become dear to us children that we wept to see them go. Only at my brother's departure did I weep as bitterly as when these strange men left us.

The teacher had now made good his threat. By now we had no communications with America. We no longer received the monthly check from Father. As a result we were actually in want and Mother could not pay our tuition. Curtly, the teacher ordered Brother and me to stay home. We were overjoyed by this good fortune, and daily we watched the German troops passing our town.

An endless stream of troops followed the departure of the soldiers from the town. Day and night the heavy rumblings of the artillery over the cobbled stones resounded. Cavalry and infantry followed in profusion. Then came countless transport wagons.

After two weeks of action, noise, and general hubbub, everything became quiet again. Not a soldier was left behind. The people of the town could not get accustomed to this stillness. Somehow business lagged, the people started going about in their old ways, sidewalks were no longer cleaned, the gutters were again full of unsanitary waste.

During the summer months of 1918, the whole town suffered from lack of food. Our family, like the other few families whose providers were in America, suffered the most. We children were yet small. Although we three boys worked from early dawn to sundown at rope making and Mother and Sister knitted sweaters and stockings for others, we still did not make enough for a bare subsistence. Many times kind neighbors brought in some stale bread that they no longer cared to eat. From our earnings and. these contributions we managed to live through that summer.

One day a family that was still well to do celebrated a birthday of one of their children. I happened to be in the house on an errand and received a slice of cake. This rare delicacy I took home. Mother cut it into four pieces and divided it among us children. We did not allow ourselves to eat the cake in an ordinary way. Instead, we took into our mouths small pieces of cake and like meat, we ate it with the stale bread. This for us was the best meal in many months, for previously our meals had consisted of stale bread alone.

It was early in November. Rumors circulated that peace had been declared. Several times during the hard summer such reports had been around. Then, the people rejoiced. They thought of the better days that would come. This joy had not lasted long, however, for the reports had proved to be false. The people of our town, therefore, failed to get excited over this new report of peace. But these rumors failed to die out as quickly as those in the summer.

Nevertheless, the people were still skeptical. They questioned what had become of all the Germans. Had all these fine men been killed? We still could not forget the life they had brought to the stricken town. Surely, if peace had been declared, the Germans would return this way; and, as yet, we had seen no vestige of them.

Our doubts were soon precipitated. About the middle of November the great German army raced homeward. The regiments seemed to vie with each other to see which one would get home first. There was no order now. Five orderly columns of marching soldiers were not to be seen. Infantry, cavalry, artillery, all were mixed. Now a detached part of artillery rushed through the town; close on its heels a few infantrymen raced by; following them, and overtaking them at a little distance, several cavalrymen flew by. Day and night this mad rush of men for home went on. The soldiers left behind cannon, heavy baggage, and packs. They would not be hindered by such cumbersome things. What had become of those wonderful bands that entertained us? Of the many bands that passed our town in the early summer, not one passed back. The soldiers had no need for bands now. They were in haste to get home to their place of residence, their wives, children, and old parents.

It took only a week for the multitude of soldiers to pass our town. When they were advancing, this army took several weeks to go through. It is striking how slow man proceeds to what he is almost sure is to be his death place. On the contrary, man runs at top speed to peace, family, and home. It is a shame that the world does not realize this and does not do away with the horror called War.

Two days had elapsed since the last German had left our town. We did not know whether more Germans would follow. As it was, we wondered under whose jurisdiction we now were. If peace had been declared, as had been reported, would we come under the jurisdiction of Russia or Germany? We were utterly ignorant of the arrangements, if any. On the third day after the German evacuation of the town, a few Russian soldiers, known as Bolsheviks, entered the town.

CHAPTER VIII
BOOTLEGGERS

The Bolsheviki's appearance did not alleviate our family's suffering. More than a year had passed now without our receiving any help from Father in America. In the first place the Germans did not allow any American mail to pass through; then the Bolsheviki, who also were not on friendly terms with America, opened all the American mail and then failed to pass it on to the person to whom it was sent.

It was impossible to obtain any work to earn our food. We children were small and could not find employment at a time when adults gladly worked for whatever the employer paid, and so men got our jobs as rope-makers. Mother tried to do housework for different families, but most of the people in town were now relatively poor, and each woman did her own housework. Knitting of sweaters for others also gave out.

Every day we three boys went around from house to house asking for some work around the house to earn enough for food. In those days we thought not of clothing. We were satisfied with garments made of sugar sacks. Our footwear consisted of rags tied around haphazardly. Some days we went from house to house and could not find any work. This meant that we went foodless to bed, hoping that the next day we would be luckier. Other days a kind woman or two would agree to let us bring her water from the well outside the town or chop some wood for heating the house or for cooking. Our remuneration consisted of a few pieces of black stale bread, and every now and then we were lucky to get a lump of sugar. Sugar was now a luxury. In the ordinary house sugar had not been used for months. It was so costly that only the very wealthy could afford its use. Others were satisfied with saccharine if they had the money to buy it.

The sugar we earned would then be cut into very small pieces, the size of a fingernail. Each one of us was given a piece to take in our mouth to sweeten the tea while we drank it from our cups. We had to be careful not to get confused and swallow the piece of sugar with a draught of tea, for we would then have to drink the tea without sweetening.

The beverage we drank we still called tea. It was not even a third cousin to tea. This tea was made of carrots cut in small pieces. These small pieces of carrot were dried thoroughly in the oven. The dried pieces were then used just as actual tea to make the beverage. The color of the beverage was as rich and sometimes even richer than from the original tea. The taste, however, was the taste of carrots. To us it differed little what its taste was. So long as the color was that of tea, we called it tea.

Thus we struggled to live. In the early winter months we managed to go around sometimes earning, at other times begging, some stale bread. But as the heavy Russian snows started to come down, the rags that covered our feet could not keep the cold and wet out. We soon realized that if we would continue to stay in the house, we would either die from starvation or from the cold in our home.

The Bolsheviki, meanwhile, were busy breaking all the stills producing the famous <u>vodka</u>. The peasants could not see the sense in that. They began to complain that they could not do without the beverage. They would come to town and literally go from house to house and ask if they could get a drink. They were willing to pay handsomely for it.

Mother saw a chance to earn food and wood to heat the house. She realized that if she would get started in the bootlegging business, we would no longer have to beg black stale bread on which to exist. We were not used to living off others. And we detested our mode of living very much. But we either had to choose between pride and starvation or donated food and existence.

Much as the bootlegging business seemed to promise a decent living, Mother did not see a way to get started. Some capital was needed. We had none. For days Mother figured ways to get a small still and, the necessary substances to make the mash.

Mother at last summoned courage to go over to the local tinner. She disclosed to him our situation and implored him to make a still for us to be paid for from future profits. At first he dared not take such a risk. He said that "He did not want to get mixed up in such affairs, He feared them." Mother promised not to disclose the creator of the machine, if it should be found in her possession. When his fears on this point were allayed, he questioned the ability of Mothers paying him for the machine. He was so pessimistic that he thought the still would be seized in its first operation. And when the machine would be gone, there would be no way of earning to pay for it.

After much persuasion, he agreed to make the desired still. Early in January 1919, the machine was completed.

In the dark of the night, we three boys took a big sack and thus started out for the machine. On our way we formulated a plan whereby we should be on constant watch while we carried the machine.

we were pushed out from the tinner's house. Immediately, Sam walked ahead. He watched for people approaching us. If he should see any one approaching, he was to give two coughs to warn Harry, the older of us three, carrying the machine. At this signal, Harry would hide in a dark alley. I brought up the rear and made sure that we were not followed. The dark night covered our actions, and we carried the still home safely.

As soon as we got home, we dug a hole in the ground of one room. We then put the still in there, covered the hole with a few boards and smoothed even that spot with soil. A stranger would have had a hard time to guess that something was hidden there by just looking at that spot.

****

A week had now passed since we had obtained the machine. During this interval the mash had gotten ready for distillation.

As night drew near, we bolted the doors, pulled down the window blinds, and closed the shutters. We wanted to be sure that not even a tiny streak of light would find its way out. The turning of the mash into vodka would take most of the night. We, therefore, took all precautions to avoid the suspicions of neighbors. If they should see a streak of light late at night, they might start to question our being up so late. When every little crevice was covered, Mother went out to see that there was no light to be seen in our house.

Fearfully we removed the soil, then the boards, and carefully took out the machine. We filled it three-fourths full of mash. We were warned not to fill it completely, for it might explode when it started to boil vigorously. The huge kettle was then covered. The cover was sealed with paste, made out of flour, spread on strips of cloth. When the heat dried the paste on the cloths, it formed a perfect seal and no steam escaped from the kettle. From the middle of the cover extended a pipe, about a half-inch in diameter. To this pipe a tin tube three feet in length was attached horizontally. This connection was also sealed. Then a coiled tube immersed in a barrel of cold water was connected and sealed to the horizontal pipe. The end of the coiled tube made its appearance at the bottom of the barrel. There a bottle was placed to receive the vodka.

The still was to be operated by the heat of charcoal. When the mash in the big kettle would start boiling, the vapor would then pass off through the only outlet, the pipe. The steam would proceed through the horizontal pipe to the coiled tube in the barrel of cold water. As the vapor was cooled it would change to a liquid and in drips would run off at the end of the pipe where it would be received by a bottle. Thus were the instructions and predictions of the creator of the machine. We were anxious to see the actual operation.

When the still was finally set up, Mother sent us children to bed. She remained alone in the room of the still to feed the machine with coal. She promised to call us when the mash started boiling and the vodka started to trickle into the bottle.

Tired from the task of setting up the machine and overstrained from fears and worries, I fell asleep soon. My sleep was not sound though and soon I was troubled by horrible dreams: Somehow the soldiers got wind of our illicit business. They were at the door knocking and ordering it to be opened. I, who seemed to be alone in the house, was determined not to let them in. They broke in the door and directed their steps to the hiding place of the still. Terrified I watched them remove the soil, the boards, and when they were about to touch the still, I rushed over to them and started screaming for help.

"Iz, don't scream so," I heard the gentle voice of my sister.

When I opened my eyes my two brothers and sister surrounded me. They were awakened by my cries. After I told them of the terrible dream, we remembered that Mother was near in the next room all closed up by herself watching the still. It had seemed a long time since we had left her. We could hardly believe that it would take so long for the mash to boil.

We decided to go in. We were eager to see whether the machine was working, or was not as predicted by the tinner.

Upon opening the door our eyes started smarting from the fumes of coal. The whole interior was full of smoke, and. we could see nothing. At last our eyes got accustomed to the smoky, unventilated atmosphere. We approached the place where Mother had been left sitting. It was odd Mother did not talk to us. Was she so taken up with her work that she had not heard us come in? Did my eyes fool me or was I still dreaming? The chair that Mother had occupied was vacant!

"Mother!" we called out in frightened tones. No answer. We ran over to the chair. We wanted to make sure that our senses were not deceiving us. We stumbled over something.

Frantic, we tugged at Mother! My thoughts ran mad.

"Mother, Mother! Why don't you answer! O! Mother! Won't you open your eyes, your lips! Oh! What shall we do?"

We stifled our cries. We kissed the unconscious figure again and again. There was no response.

We were afraid to call for help. We were at a loss. The oldest of us was fifteen. Brother suggested that we take her into the next room.

Our hot tears bathed Mother's face. Clinging to her we kissed those tears away. A quarter of an hour--longer than a year--had passed. Would not our words of endearment waken her? Our tortures got more acute.

My oldest brother disappeared for a minute and came back with a bucket full of cold water. Hurriedly, he emptied the water on Mother. Wide-eyed, the rest of us watched. Mother at last opened her eyes. She looked around and was puzzled to find herself in bed in a pool of water.

Slowly, Mother revived. After resting for an hour, Mother told us to hide the infernal machine. Feverishly, we worked to hide the still from view before the dawn set in.

CHAPTER IX
BOOTLEGGING (CONTINUED)

A week had now passed since Mother had had the almost fatal accident. She had now fully recovered, although without the aid of a physician. We were afraid to call a physician for fear of being questioned too much. Had we had the money with which to pay him we would have overlooked the questioning part. That we could have gotten around somehow. A few neighbors failing to see Mother outside came in. They did not question us about Mother's sickness. Instead they answered questions themselves. They knew that Mother would have a breakdown. She worried for her children's food. And, moreover, she denied herself even a meal sufficient to give her strength. These kind neighbors brought some food that week and saved us all from starving.

The fainting did not discourage Mother in the least. I suspect that while she was still in bed recovering, she thought of ways to ventilate the room while manufacturing the vodka. As soon as she was able to go outside, she procured a man to build a chimney out of the room used for distilling. I could never find out where Mother obtained the funds to pay for the chimney. It may be that this man was to be paid out of future gains also.

When another attempt to turn the mash into vodka was made, it proved to be a success. The fumes no longer endangered Mother's life. This time we did not want to go to bed and leave Mother alone. We all stayed up and waited for the vodka, our would-be food giver, to start dripping into the bottle. We all tasted it, and we were glad that it tasted like vodka.

To obtain the first ten customers was a real hardship. For several days Mother went out into the market place, but hesitated to ask the peasants to come for a precious drink. This was all new to her. The trade was beset with dangers. She feared lest one of the peasants would tell the soldiers. Then all the hard work, worries, and fears before the vodka was manufactured would be for nothing.

On the fifth day of her visits to the market place in quest of customers, Mother took one of the children along and that was I. She figured that even the most hardboiled peasant would hesitate to report to the soldiers our illicit traffic, if he could behold me. I presented the most pitiful appearance. My face was drawn together from pangs of hunger. My eyes were bloodshot from constant crying for food. My body was fully wrapped in heavy sacks to help keep the cold out. My footgear was also of sacks and rags.

The two of us walked into the market place. We saw two men looking at a team of horses and bargaining over the price. We approached them and stood there waiting to see them complete the sale after which Mother intended to ask them over to our house to have a few drinks. In the extreme cold we waited for more than an hour, before they agreed upon the price.

Then Mother overheard one of them say that he would like to have some <u>vodka</u> to warm up. Mother immediately approached him and told him to follow her. Thus was the first customer obtained. Mother then realized that the peasants would not report us to the soldiers. They were embittered with the soldiers for working such hardships on them in not letting them have their favorite beverage. They were delighted to partake of the liquor and not even mentioned it to anyone that might cause trouble. After having obtained the first customer successfully, Mother ventured to ask others to come to us and within a week we had ten steady customers that visited us at least once every day.

These peasants brought others and within a month we were patronized by nearly a hundred people. We got a reputation of giving the real stuff. Our <u>vodka</u> was not mixed with water, as other bootleggers were wont to do.

This business got to be profitable. In a few weeks the still was paid for. We no longer went to bed without supper. Food was plentiful. Mother even ordered us some real honest—to—goodness clothes. The only cloud that marred our enjoyment of plentiful food was the fear of a raid by the soldiers.

Several joints had been already raided. The soldiers had swooped down unexpectedly. They had beaten in the doors and had broken everything in the place. Not only had they destroyed the stills, barrels of mash, and bottles of <u>vodka,</u> but they had broken all the furniture in the house. In addition to that, they had flogged the men operating the places to unconsciousness. When we heard of these brutalities, we lived in constant fear. We did not give up our illicit traffic, however. It was better to be fed and live in fear, than to be hungry and not know of fear. We could at least hope that they would not get wind of our bootlegging. Whereas, if we were not manufacturing <u>vodka,</u> we had no hope that we would get food.

Our family had not been in bed for an hour when we were awakened by a loud pounding on the front door on a cold February night.

"Otwaretie!"--"Open up" came a command from the outside. We were paralyzed with fear. A cold sweat covered my whole body as I recollected the flogging of another bootlegger. Will Mother and we four children be treated likewise? If there had been at least one older male in the house, we would have had more confidence. He would have been able to cope more readily with such a situation.

In these few trying seconds, Mother had formed a plan to outwit the soldiers. "Harry, grab the five gallon bottle with <u>vodka</u> and, take it through the back door to the nearby cemetery." Mother was hoping that the soldiers would not be at the back door since most of the houses of this town had only one door. Our house was one of the few in town with a back door.

With lightning speed, Harry wrapped himself in an overcoat, pulled his boots on and was out with the evidence. We were fortunate not to have had any barrels with mash. The mash had been distilled the previous day. The barrels as usual had been cleaned and allowed to air for a day. Just as Brother got out the back door, Mother opened the front door to admit the soldiers.

They were surprised to see the door open for them to come in. They were accustomed to making their entry by brute strength. The mere compliance in this respect with their commands to let them in softened them and they were less harsh as they entered. They had had no time to work themselves up into a fury by breaking in the door. Furthermore, the appearance of a woman at the unbolting of the door somewhat broke their morale.

The leader began to ask questions. Where was the man of the house? How many children she had? At this question Mother hesitated a little. She gave him the right number, however, hoping that Harry would return before they started to search the house. How she provided a living for us? Kind neighbors helped us by letting Mother wash their floors and laundry was the explanation.

Before the questioning was over Harry joined us children in the bedroom. Together we listened to the cruel grilling of the soldiers. At last they exhausted their supply of questions. One of them suggested that they look around in the house.

They came into the bedroom and first looked at our wide-awake, frightened faces. They joked with us "Your father is in America making many dollars and you starve here." We answered them not. We feared lest they discover the still buried in a corner of the bedroom. They were occupied too much with us to search close enough. Two of them went into the third room, followed by Mother. They were puzzled by the empty barrels, but were finally satisfied with Mother's explanations. Good humouredly they warned Mother not to engage in the illicit manufacture of <u>vodka</u>. "We will surprise you once again," they added as they left.

Half an hour after their departure, Brother cautiously went out through the back door. Within a few minutes, he returned with the precious beverage, the liquor that meant food for us.

The next day the regular customers came for a drink. The first drinker, however, showed a puzzled face. "Are you trying to have some fun with us?" he countered. "Why, this is nothing but water." Mother was surprised at this. The <u>vodka</u> came from the five-gallon bottle. She tasted some and was convinced of the man's complaints; the beverage was plain water.

Could the extreme cold have had some effect on the <u>vodka?</u> Never before did we hear of a liquor being changed by cold. If hot had no effect on the beverage when it was being distilled, neither would cold cause a reaction. The only plausible explanation was that someone saw Brother leave the bottle in the cemetery. When he had left the liquor, it was drained and replaced with water. Whatever the explanation it was hard for Mother to convince the customers that came daily. It looked as if we were going to lose all of the patrons, for it took a full week before the mash was ready for distillation. Our reputation of giving <u>good</u> <u>stuff</u> fortunately helped us. In a month the trade was normal again.

During the month, the soldiers did not molest us. Our patrons, men and women peasants came daily and at the accustomed rap on the door, were allowed to enter. They liked to come in groups and sit around a table with a quart in front of them. Thus they would drink and chat and occasionally eat onions with salt. Then they would drink more until the bottle was empty and then order another bottle. I was always interested to see them gulp a glass full of foaming burning <u>vodka</u>--men and women alike--without even making a grimace. Their throats must have been so parched from their habitual drinking, I thought, that the drinking no longer affected them.

After a group of four or five had drunk two quarts, they would leave. These peasants never seemed drunk. No matter how much they drank, it seemed to affect them as plain water would. They had no difficulty in leaving the table. They scorned any aid. They never tottered. Only their breath indicated that they had been drinking. Watching them walk one could never tell that they were full of gin.

On a March day of 1919, a group of our patrons were celebrating at our table. As was always the case, when they were warmed up by their favorite drink, they were merry and talkative. The two men and two women at the table had finished one quart and had requested another. Mother was handing the bottle to them when there was a loud knocking, intervalled with shouts ordering to open up.

We recognized it as different from the accustomed rap of a patron. We all were very quiet and did not answer them. Mother hoped that they would knock awhile and depart.

But to our dismay they began breaking in the door. In a few short minutes a group of enraged soldiers leaped upon the peasants and started flogging them with their long lashes. Protesting loudly at this treatment, our patrons fled. The soldiers were content to let them go.

After having spent some of their fury on the poor peasants, the soldiers started to search the house. They found <u>vodka</u>, which they immediately spilled. Then they poured the mash from the barrels. This all did not satisfy them; they demanded the still. Mother refused to tell them its hiding place. They found nothing and threatened to imprison all of us. They did not refrain from using ungentlemanly language, but they never raised a hand against us.

They searched again and threatened again with no results. "Next time we will come when you manufacture the stuff. Then we will break the still and make an end to this," the leader warned Mother.

While he was haranguing us thus, one of the soldiers decided to go snooping about in our bedroom. Immediately he was on his knees and with his hands removed the soil covering the boards underneath. When he noticed the boards, he called the other soldiers to come to aid him.

In a short time they unearthed the huge kettle. With the butts of their rifles they broke the machine before our eyes. We cried bitterly. To us it was as if they were beating to death a friend, a friend that had been our provider for the last few months. This friend had seen to it that we should not be in want. Now the friend was being beaten to death!

CHAPTER X
PETLURA

Petlura! This name still makes me shudder! It horrifies me, although the man is now unable to harm me. In the spring of 1919 this name typified cruel murders, robberies, and other atrocious crimes on an innocent people in Russia. There was not a single town in southern Russia known as the Ukraine that did not live through a pogrom inspired by this bestial bandit. I could almost say that there was not a single Jewish family in the Ukraine who escaped the clutches of this beast and his lawless band. If there were no casualties in the immediate family, some poor second or third cousin or uncle or aunt suffered at the hands of Petlura.

Petlura organized his so-called army to wrest Ukraine from the Bolsheviki's hands and to organize a separate government. It was often rumored that he was financed by the Allies. The Allies did not so much care for Ukraine or Poland or Rumania to have independent governments. But they did want to break the Bolsheviki's power. By financing unscrupulous leaders the Allies could sit back and chuckle at the plaguing of the Bolsheviki by these thorns. So long as this kept the Bolsheviki busy and interfered with their getting on their feet it satisfied the powers of the world.

Petlura, however, did not show great fervor for freeing his beloved Ukraine. He displayed greater zeal in torturing and killing innocent Jews. Whether the rumored financial backers stipulated the killing of Jews, as part of their contract with Petlura was not known. Even if they did not ask him to do this very thing, they never apparently discouraged him in his bestial pursuits. That the whole world was aware of Petlura's misdeeds we had no doubts. For such wholesale slaughtering even if it occurred in uncivilized Russia, surely was given some publicity. Yet we received no relief.

Petlura made a dramatic entrance into our town. He waged an honest-to-goodness battle with Trotzky's army to get possession of <u>Minkovitz</u>. We, too, had to witness the gruesome business of men killing each other.

The Bolsheviki's stand in our town somewhat disconcerted Petlura. Previous to his approach toward <u>Minkovitz</u>, the Bolsheviki gave way easily at signs of the lawless leader and his band. They would exchange a few shot--a sort of guerilla warfar--and then leave the town to Petlura. Here, on the hills, where the Bolsheviki had the trenches made by the Czar's army, they made a stand.

*Note: Simon Petlura was shot on May 25, 1926, in Paris by a Russian student whose family died at the hands of the bandit. The assassin was arrested, and money for his defense was raised by the National Jewish Workers Alliance of New York. The trial of Schwartz Bard was not held until October, 1927 when he was finally acquitted.

The spring of 1919 came unusually early. In the early days of March the snow started melting away and warm weather prevailed. By the middle of that month no sign of winter was left. The grass grew green, and some trees started to bud. In this balmy weather, Petlura made his appearance.

Immediately, Trotsky's army took possession of the hill opposite the direction of the lawless band's approach. Before all the soldiers had left the town the Bolsheviki began cannonading over it to prevent Petlura from entering.

The first shot took us by surprise. We were totally unprepared for it. Furthermore, the shot was very strange to us. Never before had we seen actual cannon in action. When the Germans advanced we heard certain far-off cannonading. But that was a whisper compared to the report that day.

The first report was soon followed by others. That day happened to be a market day. The town was full of people selling and buying wares. As the shots were repeated, the people and animals became panic-stricken. Hurriedly, the shop—keepers began closing their shops. Parents ran in all directions calling their children. Children, frightened and crying, rushed from the dismissed school. Horses, unaccustomed to this strange noise, wildly stampeded over every one in their path. Dogs howled, as if the world were at an end. Everything was in a babel.

Before long Petlura's band started a battery of artillery going on the opposite hill. Now projectiles kept flying over the town in both directions. Boom! Boom! Thundered the guns. Vizzzz! whistled the shells as they flew from one hill to the other.

The noise of the guns soon drowned out the general uproar of the people and animals. In a very short time the crowded streets were empty. The people had filled all the available cellars in the town; the animals apparently found refuge in the numerous narrow alleys. Not a person bothered with these poor animals; everyone looked out for his own safety. The streets became unbearably quiet. In the cellars we heard only the repeated reports of the guns and the constant whistling of the shells overhead.

Squatting on the damp ground of the cellar, we sat crowded together. There was not enough room to stretch out our legs. As the bombardment continued throughout the day our crouching positions became unendurable. Standing up was the only relief we could get. Yet to most of us this relief was even worse than the squatting on the ground. Only a few had the good fortune to sit beside the walls. When they stood up, they leaned against the wall for support. But we in the center found no relief in standing up. We found it very difficult to stand for a while in a small allotted space with nothing to support us and so we endured the torturous squatting for a whole day.

Each person was engaged in his own thoughts. No one complained of the physical suffering, nor did any one talk about his mental tortures. A deadly quiet prevailed within, a quiet that could drive a person crazy. The grave and solemn faces showed that each individual was fighting insanity; each person was communing with God. The mere fact that they were taken up with spiritual things instead of material things saved the minds of many.

It is fortunate that in danger our thoughts are immediately turned to God. No matter how atheistic an individual may be in ordinary times, that person becomes religious when he finds himself in a situation from which no action of his own can rescue him. Although unconscious of the fact, that person is then as devout and earnest in his prayers as one who practices religion all his life. The ability of the human to think of something other than the immediate danger often saves his mind from going to pieces.

When night came, our bodies might have been weak and tired but our minds were sound and, fresh. Now that the cannonading had subsided, we again thought of food.

Several men went out. Within a half hour they returned and reported that no damage had been done to the town. Whether one of the combatant armies had withdrawn they could not tell, for the hillsides occupied by the soldiers were in complete darkness. The food they brought heartened us more. After eating we were at least better prepared to endure the dark night.

Early in the morning the shooting was resumed. The men, however, could no longer stay in this depressing place. Since on the previous day no harm was done to the town, they reasoned it was obvious that the armies were intent only upon destroying each other.

Emboldened by these observations, the men started going out into the streets while the shells were still flying overhead. When they came back, they told us that they drew water from the wells to give to the cows and horses who had gone without food or drink since the shooting began.

Towards night of the second day of warfare all decided to return to their houses. It seemed foolish for us to lie in a damp, crowded cellar when we could be apparently just as safe in the houses. That night we slept soundly enough in our beds.

On the third day, the shooting was as heavy as on the first. Neither side slackened up. Perhaps, the blood that had already been shed was not enough.

Each family now stayed in its own house. The men kept going out and coming back as on the previous day. Through the windows we could see them walk in twos, little minding the flying shells.

We boys became impatient and sneaked out of the house. Not far from our house we saw a group of boys of our own age sitting on a porch that gave full view of the two hillsides.

We joined them and excitedly watched the fight. "Look! Look at that shell coming from Petlura," cried one boy. "Why it raised a big cloud of dust."

In a few moments the cloud had cleared away.

"See those Bolsheviki crawling on their belies," shouted another. "They must have been hurt."

Petlura's shells became more numerous. The other side showed its protest by a few scattered shots. It obviously felt safe enough on its hillside, and showed no signs of retreating.

Darkness put an end to the third day of warfare. Only the dawn of the next day would reveal whether the fighting would continue. Although we had now got accustomed to the earsplitting reports, we, nevertheless, wished very much that an end would come to this struggle.

Early in the morning of the fourth day, the hillside of the Bolsheviki was vacated. Petlura's band sent over a few shells to the now quiet hillside. They received no answer. In half an hour, the town was full of Petlurzas--our town's official name for this lawless band.

These soldiers did not come in orderly lines. They rushed into town like a mob of people carried away by their emotions. These soldiers fairly ran into town. We wondered how such an undisciplined band could battle with Trotzky's army. How they could be kept at their posts while fighting. Most of these soldiers were young boys from the nearby villages. These boys had been lured by the leader's promise to rob the Jews. Only the desire to confiscate the wealth of the Jews kept them together.

Their appearance was shocking. Nearly all of them were hatless. Their unkempt hair was made more hideous by the breeze. Each soldier's dirty face was fertile with bristles. Not one of them had on a decent garment. Most of them were clad in a heavy linen shirt and a pair of trousers. Only the linen shirts, once white, presented the appearance of some uniformity; not two pairs of trousers were alike; if they once were, the many patches on them now covered up that fact. Rags wound around the feet formed most of the men's footgear.

The officers and orderlies boasted the same raiment. We at first did not know which were their leaders. Upon looking more closely, however, we noticed a few with revolvers at their sides. These, we assumed, were the officers. The majority carried rifles with bayonets attached.

As soon as the men reached the town, they swarmed into the houses and demanded food. Four bums, among them a lad from a nearby village, entered our house. "Give us something to eat," was the order of the boy known by Mother.

"Ivan, you know that we haven't any bread for ourselves." A blow on mother's face by the brute's open hand warned her not to plead with him.

The four started a search of the house for food. Soon they became enraged because they could not find any. "Dirty Jews," they cursed, "you had hidden all of your food before we came. We'll get even with you before we leave."

Although they did not find food, they nevertheless decided to stay with us. Two went out to get food from another "damn Jew," while the remaining two, unwashed, lay down, each in a bed, to rest from the recent hardship.

When night came, the intruders refused to give up the only two beds in the house. We begged them for a pillow. For an answer, the boy from the neighboring town jumped out of bed and with his belt began striking us over the faces and bodies. On that night and on the nights of the following month, the bare ground served as our beds.

Those four soldiers were the most filthy people I ever encountered. They were, as it seemed, afraid of water. I never saw them wash their hands, faces, or heads. Their bodies, I have no doubt, had not felt any water since the preceding summer when they might have gone swimming in the river. The shirts they had on were black with dirt. During the whole month that they stayed in our town, they did not even once wash these shirts. They could not, however, endure the constant torture of the many lice that fed and fattened upon their dirty bodies. Every other day the four soldiers took their things off and got busy killing the insects by pressing the nails of the two thumbs together. It sickened us to watch them do this. But because of their supremacy we could not escape from the house. They locked the doors and then distributed themselves in the three rooms. Thus, no matter to what room we fled, we found a soldier killing lice.

We were glad to see these brutes leave in April. They rested a whole month and ate almost all of the town's supply of food. When they felt strong and rested, they again set out on the warpath.

Before a month had passed, after Petlura and his band had left us, rumors began to circulate that the Bolsheviki gave Petlura's army a good beating in Zamechif, a town about thirty miles distant from our place. It was also reported that before he actually left the town, he ordered his soldiers to kill all the Jews and rob them of their wealth. This order, it was said, was carried out.

These rumors disconcerted us very much, for there is always some truth in rumors. Furthermore, we experienced Petlura's followers' behavior while they were quartered in our homes. Their cruelty was unbearable, although they were then joyous from the recent victory. We could almost believe all that was said about their pogrom, especially when they were depressed from the very recent reverses, in their warfare with the Bolsheviki.

Early in May the rumors of Petlura's pogroms were verified when Uncle Dave received a letter by messenger from his brother, who barely escaped alive from Kitarid, his hometown. It then dawned upon us that these beasts with the appearance of human beings were capable of anything, even of torturing innocent Jews to death. In this bloody work, they were aided by ignorant peasants from nearby villages. His letter continued:

Towards night, a band of soldiers entered the town. Many peasants carrying empty sacks followed them. As the soldiers reached the market place, they opened fire with several machine guns. The Jewish populace immediately rushed to their homes in which they locked themselves. Uncle's brother at that time was in a Christian home. He begged the head of the house to allow him to remain there until the pogrom would be over. The man, who was intelligent and, therefore, did not bear the ignorant Christians' hatred toward the Jews, permitted him to stay. He even went out to dissuade, if possible, the peasants from participating in the attack.

One of the boys of the house stationed himself on the doorpost to prevent the pillagers from entering by telling them that Christians inhabited the house. Uncle's brother placed himself at a window, whose shade was drawn down, and through a chink watched the hideous spectacles.

Soldiers with bayonets on their rifles broke into Jewish houses. After remaining there for several minutes, they appeared again taking with them the women. The bayonets were red with blood. In one house, a young man, who apparently had showed some opposition was thrown out from a second-story window. The peasants outside did not even let him rise. They beat him to death with heavy clubs. When the soldiers left the open houses, the peasants entered them and filled their sacks with the possessions.

Half an hour after the murdering and plundering began, Uncle's brother's host returned home. He related that he and a few other friendly Christians begged the peasants and soldiers to leave the town. Their pleadings were not heard. Instead, they were threatened with their lives if they would be found interfering or quartering infidels. When the few friendly Christians realized that they could do nothing, they departed to their homes to avoid witnessing the bloody work.

The soldiers committed the most brutal crimes. When they entered a house which men and elderly women inhabited, they gored the men and led the women to the big synagogue where they locked them in with other unfortunates. When, however, they entered a house in which there were young girls, they tied the hands and feet of the whole family. Then they gagged the girls. Each brute then took his turn in attacking the young innocent girls in front of the entire helpless family. After performing this fiendish act, they killed all the family except the girls, whom they left gagged and unconscious.

When night at last came, Uncle's brother hoped that the darkness would put an end to the butchery. This hope was short-lived, for as soon as it got dark, the sky lighted up with fire. His host, after a brief absence, returned with the sorrowful news that the synagogue with the many women in it was being burned.

In the morning, when the human beasts had left town, Uncle Dave's brother went home. The windows of the house were broken; the doors were off the hinges. Inside, covered with feathers, lay his murdered father. Frantically, he ran to his relatives to find his mother's whereabouts. Their homes presented the same picture. He then rushed to the big synagogue. A heap of ruins remained there. Nothing more.

Petlura repeated these crimes in almost every town he entered, In the meanwhile, the Bolsheviki came ever closer to the fleeing band. By the time Petlura reached our town, he was too much afraid of an attack by the pressing Bolsheviki to start a general slaughter of the Jews. His followers, as they went by had to be content with a few scattered shots into the houses of the Jews. Two men were injured——not seriously, by these stray bullets.

Hardly had Petlura left the town when Trotsky's army, after a month's absence, once more made its appearance.

CHAPTER XI
STARVING

The early part of summer of 1919 was the hardest for our family. Nearly every day in June and July we faced starvation. There was not a day in the two months that we were certain of our food. Each day we were presented with problems of obtaining something to eat in order to keep from starving. In those days we never worried for the morrow for to exist TODAY was the problem.

There was no place to earn anything in those trying days. Only the oldest brother was learning the tailoring trade. For payment, he received his daily food. He was content with this. If he had refused these terms, he would have had to stay at home and starve, with us.

We had the greatest difficulty to obtain some little food to prevent our strength from ebbing away. Each morning, Mother and Sister went from house to house asking for any kind of housework to earn the day's load. Nearly each morning they were unsuccessful in their quest.

When noon came and hunger began to gnaw at them, they started to make the rounds among the farmers close to the town. After visiting about a dozen farmhouses they would return with about four or five potatoes-- enough to still our hunger for the day.

Once we tried to eat the potatoes raw, since we had no wood with which to roast them; but we could not eat them raw. Then, Sam suggested that he and I go out in the streets and gather dead limbs that had fallen from trees, small chips, and splinters with which to roast the potatoes. Daily we two went all over the town collecting chips of wood in a sack, hoping that Mother and Sister would bring some food.

Occasionally they brought a little cornmeal. Then, Mother would cook a mush from it. Although the mush lacked salt--a priceless thing in those days--to give it the right taste, we nevertheless enjoyed the small repast as if it were a feast.

Not on every day could food be obtained. Days, Mother and Sister came home empty-handed; on such days we lived on water alone. The water-days were about as frequent as the food-days.

Our oldest brother could no longer see us suffer. He told us that he could not enjoy his meals, for he was reminded of our empty stomachs just as he started to eat. He, therefore, suggested that he go to the nearby villages. There he would do tailoring for the peasants. In return for his work he would ask for flour. The flour would at least give us bread to sustain ourselves.

Mother objected to this plan. She feared lest misfortune should befall him. The roads were infested with highwaymen. These bandits robbed and killed people going from one town to another. Three murdered men from our town were found on the highway. Their hands and feet had been bound, and their throats had been slashed open. Mother, therefore, was loath to allow a lad of eighteen to endanger himself for our sakes. It was known that the bandits slashed all their victims' throats, whether the unfortunate travelers had money on their persons or not.

Brother, however, insisted that the village to which he intended to go could be reached by a by-way, which the bandits did not frequent. At last Mother allowed him to go in the company of an older man, who also went to the village to earn food for his family by tailoring. Each, however, was to pursue his own way as soon as they reached the village.

The two were gone for two weeks. For fourteen days we were worried about Harry's safety, for we could get no word from him. He had no way of letting us know, for the postal system was broken down, and mail could neither be sent nor received. Only when he returned would we know that he was safe and alive. Before leaving, he said he would not be back within two weeks.

On the fourteenth day, Sam and I walked out on the road by which Harry was to return. There we hoped to relieve him of his burden--the flour that he would receive for his work. After a mile's walk, we feared to advance farther. On the side of the road, we sat down to wait for Brother to make his appearance. About three o'clock in the afternoon the two came into view. Each carried a small, filled bag. From the bag's size, we could tell that Brother did not need our aid. Its probable weight was about ten pounds.

How good it was to look at the flour, to feel it, and to let it run through our fingers to make sure that it was flour. For more than two months we had not seen any wheat-flour. We had almost forgotten how it looked. Now we were overjoyed with this small sack of flour. It meant bread. It meant food. We asked not for other delicacies so long as we had bread to quiet our hunger.

Our thoughts tricked us, though. The flour suggested bread. But how the bread would be baked slipped our minds altogether. Only when Mother said that there was no wood with which to bake the bread did we realize that we were no closer to bread than we had been a day or a week before. We had no money to buy wood, and to go out in the streets to pick up small chips and splinters would not have been sensible. To roast a few potatoes we could find chips enough. But to heat an oven for the baking of bread required solid wood, not mere chips and splinters.

"Let's break the chicken-coop and bake the bread with its wood." suggested Harry. This sounded sensible. We were certain that in the near future we would own no chickens. And when the time should come when we would own chickens, we would probably then be able to make another coop. We were concerned with the present. The wood from the coop would help quiet our hunger, and so we lost no time in breaking the coop to bake the salt-less bread.

Never did bread taste any better. We could not have eaten the best cake with such a relish. Although without salt, we nevertheless, enjoyed this bread better than we had the best food formerly. I could then empathize with the Children of Israel, who had had no other food in the desert but manna. The manna to them tasted like meat or any other food of which they happened to think while they had been partaking of the desert food. We, too, enjoyed our black bread. The bread was still hot when Mother gave each of us a piece. I took in my mouth tiny bits of bread. I feared that I would not quiet my hunger if I took in large lumps. Just holding the bread in my hand, looking at it, and thinking that this dark mess would keep me from starving for at least the coming day or two helped to make me feel less hungry. When I, at last, finished my portion of bread, I was at peace with the world and bore no ill will towards any person.

Harry soon saw that the few loaves of bread would not last the four of us for the two weeks that he would be away. He, therefore, suggested that Sam and I accompany him to the village. There he would set us to work ripping coats, pants, and other articles of clothing. These ripped clothes were then made into what looked to be like new garments. In reality, they were turned inside out. Since the inside pattern of the material was always different from the outside pattern, they presented the appearance of new garments. The peasants had to be content with these suits, since there were no new materials to be had for any price. Occasionally Harry made a new blouse for one of the wealthier peasants who had home-made linen.

Since Sam and I performed some work, the peasants did not object to our staying and eating at their houses. The first day we came to the Village, we nearly died from over-eating. For the first time in a year, we saw before us a table full of food. Potatoes, cucumbers, green onions green garlic, sweet corns, milk, cream, butter, and bread all beckoned to us to partake of them. We could not refuse their hospitality, and we ate of everything. But before the day was over, we were rolling on our backs with the worst stomachache. We were more cautious, however in the days that followed.

For a month, we stayed in the country with Brother. At the end of every two weeks we went home. We would then take along the little flour that Harry had earned so that Mother and Sister would have enough to eat. The chicken- coop provided wood for the whole month. When we came home at the end of August, Mother informed us that there was no more wood with which to bake the bread. That meant that Mother and Sister would not have any food. Upon hearing this news, Harry made no comment. I was sure that before Mother would finish telling us about having no wood, Harry would already have a suggestion whereby to obtain some. To my surprise, however, he said nothing.

As the sun began to set that day, Harry called Sam and me aside. He explained that what occurred to him that we might be able to get some wood from the forest that was two miles distant from the town. He said he had noticed that the peasants brought home wood from the forest nearly every night. He, therefore, was sure that we could get some too. He was certain that no one was guarding the forest at that time. The only difference between the peasants and us was that they had a wagon and horses to draw the wood home; we would take as much as we could carry and if we succeeded we could repeat our visits to the forest on subsequent weeks. This appealed to us. Furthermore, we wanted to be sure that Mother and Sister had enough to eat while we were away. And we agreed to his suggestion.

When it got dark, I sneaked in to Grandfather's and got his blunt ax. I dared not ask him for it, for I was sure if I told him for what we would use the ax, he would stop us from going. Harry put the ax in a sack, so that nobody would see us carry it while we left the town. Barefoot, we started walking to the forest. We went through alleys so that no one would see us leave.

In less than half an hour we reached the outskirts of the woods. We looked around us; we saw no one near. We looked above and we saw black clouds covering the shimmery light of the stars. This did not discourage us. We were sure that we would get the wood to bring home as a surprise to Mother.

The ax was taken out from its hiding place, and when we got accustomed to the dark forest we looked around for young trees which our dull ax would be able to chop down. Harry started chopping at a young tree, but it yielded not to our ax. At each stroke the sapling bent down and rebounded again. It seemed as if we would have to return without wood. But Brother would not yield, with great efforts, the three of us bent down to the ground the unyielding tree. While Sam and I held it down, Harry with much effort succeeded in separating it from its root.

We were thus engaged on the second sapling when flashes of lightning, followed by reports of thunder, were seen. Immediately the skies opened and poured out a heavy rain. For half an hour we crouched under a huge oak. But the tree did not protect us from the heavy downpour. Our clothes dripped from the rain as much as did the overtaxed branches of the trees. At last the rain stopped, and we proceeded with our enterprise.

After much hard work, we succeeded in chopping down four trees. The night had meanwhile advanced; we, therefore, abandoned the original plan of cutting the trees into small blocks, which tied together with a rope could have been carried on our backs. Instead, we decided to pull the saplings home. Harry took two. To the one that *Sam* was to pull he fastened Grandpa's ax so that it would not be in the way, while I placed the fourth tree on my shoulder, and we started the long pull in the mud, formed by the recent downpour.

Under our heavy burdens, which were growing heavier as the mud constantly kept gathering on the ends of our loads, we had crawled about half a mile, when out of the darkness appeared two figures.

"Stop' commanded one of them.

As the two came closer, we made out that it was a young man and a girl. They were apparently young lovers enjoying themselves in the complete darkness where no one could interfere with them. When as they approached us, they were walking arm in arm. Our pitiful figures bent under our heavy loads did not disconcert them. They were certain that we would not be able to learn their identity in the pitch darkness after a rain.

The young man, who, no doubt wanted to show off before his sweetheart, pulled out a revolver and ordered us to drop the wood. "I suppose the right thing for me to do would be to tie you three dogs to trees and drill you to death," he taunted us, as we shivered from wet and fear. "But," he added with a kind gesture, "I'll let you off easy this time. Run along home and don't return again."

As we took to our heels, he sent a few bullets after us and roared with laughter. The mud was too slippery, and each of us fell several times and got muddy from head to foot before we reached the open highway that was paved with cobblestones. Even on the highway we dared not slow down. At the same rapid pace, we ran into town.

At home Mother had been worried about our safety. She could not account for our being out so late. When we three, muddy, and out-of-breath, ran into the house, she almost fainted at our shocking appearance. After regaining our breath, but with much sobbing, we related what had happened to us. And we added that she better not tell Grandpa that we had lost his ax, or else we would be in for a beating for taking it without his consent.

The following week, the three of us again left for the country. This was the first week since Brother began working in the village that no bread had remained at home for Mother and Sister. Every time I sat down to eat in the village, I nearly choked thinking of the two beloved at home hungering. Not for want of flour but for lack of wood. Neither did my brothers enjoy their meals. They, too, left their food almost untouched.

When the week's work was finished, Brother Harry asked the peasants to give him less flour. He implored them, however, to give him in addition to the flour some money. After the kindly peasants had heard of our difficulties in obtaining wood, they gave us some money.

That weekend we started for home with a quicker pace. We were anxious to get borne. This time we brought money with which to buy wood, as well as flour for bread. For once, at least, we were certain that we would not have to leave Mother and Sister behind to hunger when we returned to the village again the subsequent week.

During the whole of that summer, we three made bi-weekly excursions to the countries around about our town. Every once in a while Brother Harry's first companion and guardian to the village would walk home with us. Very rarely, however, did he accompany us to the country.

One week-end late in September, this man walked home with us. The man whose age was about thirty was, nevertheless, fairly small; his height was not much more than four feet six inches. Indeed, his head seemed so large for his shoulders that we always wondered how his thin narrow shoulders--he had no neck worth speaking o--could endure the weight of such a head. To burden his poor shoulders the more, he had on a big heavy cap in that warm September day.

The day was unusually hot for that time of the year. We all walked barefoot. Brother Sam and I did not have any footgear at all. Brother Harry had a pair of boots, but he did not wear them while walking to and from the village. When we left the town, he took off his boots and then put them on again when we entered the town. Tied together, the boots thrown over Sam's shoulder were being carried home. In like manner, I carried the man's boots, while be and Harry each carried the visible earnings--the flour.

Thus the four of us trudged along. Leisurely, we approached the main highway upon which we still had a half-mile's walk before entering the town. As we got closer to the cobbled highway, even before we could actually see it, we heard dull rumblings coming from that direction. We soon could distinguish this noise. The repeated heavy rumblings suggested to us the moving of heavy artillery. We had heard that sound enough times to recognize it now easily.

We were at a loss to account for the moving of the artillery. We did not know whether it meant retreat or advance. The village in which we worked always was two to three weeks behind in the news. Since it was not on the highway, news trickled through to it very slowly. As a result, we never knew what was going on in the towns.

Therefore, we quickened our steps as we heard these dead rumblings. During the half hour, which it took us to reach the highway, the rumblings continued. When we, at last, caught sight of the road, we realized that we had guessed right.

Heavy cannons each drawn by three teams of horses, were being hurried over the cobblestones at great speed. The manner in which they speeded seemed to indicate that the enemy was on their heels, for, as we got closer, we could see that the Bolsheviki were fleeing to dear old Moscow again.

This sight disturbed our thoughts a great deal. We had enjoyed several months of peace. Although we suffered much from hunger, at least we had had no fear of being butchered as we had had when Petlura and his band roamed in our towns. It was true that the Bolsheviki had not alleviated our sufferings from hunger; yet, they had not burdened us with mental agonies of being killed and robbed, or of dishonoring our girls. The officers had been very scrupulous about the soldiers' behavior. If at any time one or two soldiers would start going around robbing the Jewish populace in town, the guilty soldiers would soon be punished by heavy floggings in the marketplace and then put under arrest. As a result of this discipline, we had been abused very rarely. Now that they were fleeing our minds were tortured. Would the beast Petlura make his appearance again? Or would some other enemy come to torture us? With these sad thoughts we reached the highway.

Upon seeing us, a soldier jumped off of a cannon and headed towards us. As he neared us, we could see that his boots were so badly torn that his toes showed through. His clothes were also in tatters; his head was hatless. He approached Brother Sam and told him to take off the boots from his shoulder. In a few minutes, he had his torn boots off and in their place were Harry's. They seemed to fit perfectly.

"Take these, my boots, comrade," he addressed Brother Sam, "I'm only exchanging them for yours; this is fair."

This did not seem to satisfy him yet. He looked us over. Our clothes were not in a better state than his. Besides, only Brother Harry's garments would have fitted him; the rest of us were considerably shorter than the soldier. Our companion's cap fascinated him, however.

"Hand over your cap," he ordered. "Please, comrade, take my boots but leave me my cap," pleaded the victim.

"Shut your trap," shouted the soldier. He then removed the cap from our companion's head and tried it on.

At this action, our companion's face paled. I never saw a face so full of agony. It became ugly with distortion. I feared lest he faint or die. I doubted that the soldier injured him by the mere removing of the cap. Yet it seemed to me that no face could be so distorted by anything other than great physical suffering. Still, I could see no wound on his person that would cause him this agony.

The cap was too large for the soldier's head. Contemptuously he threw it back, "Keep your damn hat," and he left us.

As our companion regained his cap, his distorted face assumed its natural appearance. The cap he did not put on. Instead, he jammed it into his bosom out of sight.

"I will not risk again my few rubles that I earned this week," he explained. "You see, I sewed that money into the lining of the cap. This seemed to be the safest place. Then that damned soldier comes along and wants my cap. At the thought of losing my week's earnings, I nearly fainted. No, I better take no more chances."

CHAPTER XII
THE POLES

Two days after the Bolsheviki had vacated our town; Polish scouts came to make sure that no one was in ambush waiting for them. Only after the scouts had satisfied themselves that the town contained no more of the Red army, did the Polish army proper make its appearance. The few companies of soldiers that entered the town first presented rather a poor show. Although they were clothed well and looked to be well-fed, their fighting apparatus-- cannon and munitions--looked to be inferior to that of the Red army. I was at a loss to explain the Bolshevikites retreat. It seemed impossible that such a weak enemy as the Poles could menace and frighten such a big and well-equipped bully as the Bolsheviki.

The first day that the Poles made their appearance they developed a decided antipathy to the Jewish population of the town. Nor did they become less hostile during their several months' stay. The first thing they did when they arrived was to procure quarters for the soldiers. This they did without any scruples about the discomforts they caused hundreds of families. In three room dwellings that already contained a family of five or more, five or six soldiers were roomed. These rude soldiers had no respect for men, women, or children. They were altogether indifferent to the sufferings they caused. They demanded the beds in the houses and got them. Small children and women, to say nothing of men, had to sleep on the cold, damp, hardened earthen—floors in their own homes. The heartless soldiers did not even spare a pillow for the innocent children. No, the bare hard ground served as pillows for nearly all the Jewish population during the winter's stay of the Poles in our town.

This gave us an example of their cruelties on their arrival. The next and succeeding days, they showed us other specimens of their rude behavior.

Old orthodox-Jews allow their whiskers to grow. To them it is sacrilegious to shave or trim their beards. The Poles were well aware of this. Instead of being tolerant and allowing the Jews to follow their own customs, they made fun of them. Great was the joke to them when they clipped the whiskers of an old and helpless man. Their laughter was boisterous at this joke. For how could they resist laughing when their comrades got hold of a poor helpless Jew, and holding him by his hands and feet prostrate on the ground, would cut off a semblance that was holy to him. The Poles never got tired of this joke. They saw to it that all the old Jew's whiskers were clipped. They would not tolerate a beard.

These old men who were thus basely and shamefully treated were also targets for physical sufferings at the hands of those brutes. The Poles, who had only two years before obtained their own freedom, liked to enslave others. They especially enjoyed making old men work. Those old men whose religion was being laughed at and made fun of by ignorant Poles, were daily recruited to chop wood, carry water, and dig trenches. The helpless old Jews were treated worse than serfs. Because of their ages, they could not work as fast as their taskmaster demanded; and they were flogged with big lashes to keep them from slackening-their work. Grandpa daily came home bleeding. His face, hands, and his whole body were cut up from the continuous lashings by the brutes, who were the overseers. If an old man tried to rest for a few seconds, he got more than the usual share of floggings from the brutal soldiers.

The women and young girls also suffered much at their hands. The Poles wanted their offices to be clean. To do this work, they daily gathered scores of women and girls to wash the floors and windows of the public buildings. In the bitter cold, the women who were none too well protected from it, had to wash the windows and floors. For this work, they received no pay. Often they, too, received a few lashes over their bodies as an incentive to work faster.

This same winter the influenza epidemic broke out in our town. As a result of the bad treatment that we received at the hands of the Poles--sleeping on the cold ground, working hard in the extreme cold, and general mistreatment--we could not very well withstand the disease and many of the Jewish populace contracted the sickness.

Early in December, the epidemic began to rage. Every family had an invalid. In some families all the members were bedridden. The death rate started to mount. In a town, where one or two deaths occurred in a month, now three or four deaths took place in a week. Everyone was frightened by this calamity. Soon reports spread that if the outer walls of a house, in which there was sickness, were surrounded with a charcoal mark no deaths would occur in that house.

Within a few days after this report was made current, every house in town was so decorated. Yet, there was no relief.

The number of deaths mounted daily. We began to get accustomed to three or more funerals a day. It seemed impossible to dig enough graves for all the deceased. Since so many were sick, those that were still on their feet had to work very hard to take care of the sick--and the dead.

Our town had only one doctor. Only through a miracle did he endure that hard and trying winter. Day and night he ceaselessly kept going from house to house.

He had a cheering word for everyone. He treated the rich and poor alike. Even though the poor family could not pay him, he came around daily and attended its sick as diligently as he did his wealthy patients. He neglected his family that was also suffering from the epidemic. In fact he gave his family so little medical attention that his mother and two brothers died that fatal winter.

In January 1920 Mother and we four children took sick with the flu. Grandpa, seventy years old nursed us back to health. He attended us day and night; saw that the doctor came daily; took our temperatures; kept the ice bags in place; and nourished us with whatever food he could obtain. Grandpa's excellent nursing brought us through the crisis and we recovered.

Not everyone was lucky enough to recover. The death toll mounted daily. Everybody was at a loss to account for this sudden epidemic. Then the Rabbis said that the town was under a curse. The death toll, they said, would continue unless a wedding ceremony was performed in the cemetery. This would appease the deity that put the curse on the town and the epidemic would cease.

In those troublesome days no one thought of getting married. Even if there would have been couples ready to marry, they would not have consented to have their ceremony in the cemetery. A wedding in the cemetery was such a fantastic idea that it seemed impossible to obtain a couple willing to be wedded there. A wedding, which is always a joyous and happy affair, could not be conceived to take place in an environment of sorrow and grief. A week had passed since the Rabbis had suggested this unusual marriage, and no couples had volunteered to help rid the city of the epidemic curse. Such a novel ceremony over the graves of the recent dead appealed to no one. It seemed that such a good suggestion, to deliver so easily the town from its sickness, would have to go to waste.

The Rabbis in our town, however, believed in their pet theories. This seemed too good a theory not to be proved. Therefore, to encourage a couple to marry in the cemetery, a certain sum of money was promised to that couple. A day after this remuneration for the wedding ceremony was announced, a couple announced their readiness to go through with the strange marriage. Both the boy and girl were extremely poor. The offer meant to them a great deal. It meant that they would be able to start life together without fear of facing starvation, for at least the first two years. It also meant that if the young man would capitalize the money in some enterprise, they might have an assured income for life. Whichever way the couple looked at it, it was an opportunity worth grasping for. What if shivers would run through the spine while the ceremony took place? That would last only for an hour at the most. Then, they would enjoy life like any ordinary married couple.

The town took on a festive air for this gala occasion. All the healthy populace dressed in their best and flocked to the synagogue from where the procession would start. Within the synagogue young people danced to the tunes of music and were making merry just as if this were an ordinary wedding. To have this ceremony have the right effect the Rabbis declared that it had to take place at night. So the people enjoyed themselves dancing the whole day. At last the night came and the procession to the cemetery was ready to start.

At the head of the procession walked several men bearing torches in their hands to light the way. The musicians who played the regular wedding march were in back of the torchbearers. Then followed the Rabbis. Behind them came the couple accompanied by their parents. In back of them came a long line of the townspeople who would not miss such a wedding ceremony even when their fathers, mothers, sisters, brothers, or children were on their death-beds and. needed their aid and comfort. That wedding was attended by a record crowd--all those that were on their feet, after having weathered the terrible sickness or still not overcome by it.

The procession marched around the town before it headed for the cemetery. At last it reached the gates. There the music ceased playing and the gay spirit immediately left the crowd. Instead a somber silence settled over it.

Over several fresh graves the usual wedding-canopy was held by four young men. The oldest Rabbi of the town who was to officiate was the first one to take his place under the canopy. Then the bride and groom, after much hesitation and with tears in their eyes, were pulled under it by their parents. No one else stepped under the canopy in a regular marriage ceremony; the closest relatives of the groom and bride also stepped under the canopy and remained there until the end of the ceremony.

In the extreme cold the curious, sorrowful, silent-weeping crowd watched the arrangement under the canopy. This crowd now had occasion to recall their dear one--relatives or close friends--who had recently been lowered into the cold graves. The thought of these untimely deaths made every one present break down and weep like children. Men and women alike were weeping. The men silently wiped the tears away from their eyes; the women could not control their emotions and started crying loudly. The children soon followed the example of the older people and the previous gay and dancing crowd turned into sorrowful mourners.

Then the resonant voice of the Rabbi began to be heard. At first the prayers were delivered up in low tones. But as he warmed up to the chanting, his voice assumed a somewhat higher pitch. With his head raised, he stood motionless, except for his moving mouth, in the bitter cold and offered up to the Almighty one prayer after another.

The crowd soon forgot its grief. Spellbound, we also stood motionless as we watched this awe- inspiring personage communing, as it were, with God. We did not mind the extreme cold. In fact we did not feel it, for our minds were taken up with spiritual instead of earthly things. Even as we watched the Rabbi pray for the whole town, each one of us separately, silently, prayed that the beloved ones sick at home be spared.

Then the Rabbis praying ceased. Seven times the parents and the bride walked around the groom, standing in the middle. The Rabbi then offered up another prayer while holding a glass of wine in his hand. The groom and bride each sipped some of the wine. The glass was broken by the groom who stamped on it with his right foot. The wedding ring was placed on the bride's finger. The final benediction was given, and the two were man and wife.

The entire ceremony, which usually took from ten to fifteen minutes, lasted two hours. None of us complained of the extreme January cold while we watched. We had full faith in it and were confident that the epidemic would stop.

The day following the ceremony had as many deaths as the previous day. And in the days that followed great numbers of people died. Among the latter deaths was Grandpa. Despite the care we took of him and the excellent nursing of Mother, the flogging and hard work that the Poles had imposed on him, as on many other old and young people, had weakened him too much to be able to withstand the new enemy--the epidemic.

Early in April the flu had worked itself out. It could not cause any more harm in the town. Every house was visited by it during the winter. The result was that the town had become immune to it. During that month the town started to get on its feet again.

Chapter XIII
RECOVERY

Not once during the winter did my two brothers and I go to the village to earn our daily food. In Russia heavy snows start coming down early in the fall. That winter the snow on the ground almost never melted entirely. When a deep snow had about melted away, another storm succeeded it. Old people said that the frosts also were more severe than ever before. It may be that the frost was felt more because there was not enough wood to warm the houses, nor did we have enough clothes to keep warm while outside in the bitter cold.

Because of a lack of warm clothing, we dared not go to the country. We never could have traversed the six miles in the extreme cold. We were certain that if we started out in our scanty clothing we would freeze to death, as did many people who, unprotected against the cold, dared to start on the road that winter.

Another reason, although of less importance, for not going to the country that winter was that the Poles issued an edict that all the Jews living in villages should move to the towns. The Poles wanted more Jews to torture with taunts and heavy work. As a result of this tyrannous edict, hundreds of Jewish people had to break up their homes and move to the towns to starve and suffer with the rest of their people. The edict also forbade any Jew from entering the villages to work there. This was of less importance, because the peasants were willing to shield the Jewish workers by keeping their presence in the village a secret.

Thus very early in the winter we, along with others, started to suffer from lack of food. Our suffering, however, was not as severe as had been anticipated. In November the town received relief from America. If it had not been for that timely relief from America, that winter would have been even more disastrous to the Jews cooped in the small crowded towns. This relief provided us with food the whole winter. We also received some clothing and wooden shoes. The generous Americans saved millions from starvation—a fate that had kept facing us for years; a fate that we were now at a loss to know how to avert since the bitter cold had set in. The millions thus saved will never forget America's generosity. It will even be remembered by their children and grandchildren.

As the balmy weather of Spring set in, Brother Harry was not content to be idle and depend on the daily food parceled out from the American relief. He was anxious to go back to the villages to earn our food. It certainly was much easier to be at home and receive the daily food without any worries or trouble. But to us it was a dole. We were grateful for the help and took it when we were to choose between the dole and starvation. But when it got warmer and there was a chance of earning daily food-- although with some danger of being discovered in forbidden regions--we were glad to go out and earn it.

In this venture Brother Harry refused to take Brother Sam and me along. Instead he went into partnership with a boy of his age. Together they left on a Sunday night in early April. They were confident that they would get enough work. The Easter holidays were not far off and the peasants had not had any clothes' made during the winter. The boys were certain then to be kept busy and would earn enough the first week to keep us so that we would not have to depend on the dole.

During that week in April of 1920, the Poles started to get restless. Towards the end of the week a few detachments of Polish soldiers passed through the town in the direction of Poland. This started to worry us. We were afraid that while passing through the villages looking for wagons and horses to help them in their flight they might discover Brother and his partner.

Friday night came. The two had promised to return home that night. The long hours passed by slowly. The hour of nine came and went. The two had not yet made their appearance. Mother started to get worried over Brother's absence. She blamed herself for letting him go. Had she known that the Poles would start their flight that week she would not have let him go under any circumstances.

About ten o'clock we saw a face flat against the outside windowpane. The strain of the previous two hours caused us to jump up at this apparition. So upset were we that for a minute or two we were unable to recognize the owner of that face.

"Harry home yet?" and showing us a rooster that he carried, he fled.

When we had recognized Brother's partner, he was gone. Mother wanted to question him where Harry was; why the two did not come together. She, therefore, followed him to his house to question him.

Mother returned soon looking more worried than before. He only said that Brother had started home before him. He would not tell her why they had not come home together or whether the two had argued and separated.

About twelve o'clock, midnight, Brother made his appearance. He was all worn out. So tired was he that he nearly fell into a chair to get rested.

When he had rested sufficiently, he related the reason of his late homecoming:

The two had started from the village about eight o'clock at night. A peasant agreed to take them with his horses and wagon to the edge of the woods about two miles away from our town. There he dumped them and several sacks of potatoes--their earnings for the week. He was afraid to proceed farther for the peasants had learned of the Poles flight. They also learned that the Poles took all the horses and wagons that they could seize. If, perchance, the Poles should get a hold of his wagon and horses, it might mean months before he could get them back, if at all. Therefore, he left them at the edge of the forest, while he fled home to hide the horses and wagon.

When the two partners were thus left, Brother suggested that one of them proceed to town on foot and obtain a horse and wagon to bring the potatoes home. They agreed that Brother should go to town while the other should watch the potatoes till he arrived. Brother took on his back a half sack of potatoes to show the man whose horse and wagon be hoped to hire. He knew that if he came to the man empty-handed, the other would not believe him. When he would behold the potatoes he might be convinced and risk his horse and wagon.

With such a load, Brother made slow progress. At last he reached the man's home, got him out of bed, and started to induce him to go with him to the woods to bring the potatoes home. He had had a hard time to get the man to go. At last when Brother offered to leave the half sack of potatoes with him as a sign of good faith, the man agreed to get his horse and wagon from the hiding place and haul the potatoes home.

The two reached the place in the forest. But there was no partner and no sack of potatoes. At first Brother thought that he was not in the right place. But he soon was convinced that it was the right place, for, as they walked around looking for the partner, they stepped on hard objects that were scattered on the ground. When they examined these hard objects, they saw that they were potatoes. The potatoes were evidently scattered. But who did the scattering and where the partner had gone they could not learn.

They returned home empty-handed, for it was too dark to gather the potatoes, which were scattered over a fairly large area. When he had come into the house it was midnight. After a week's work he had come home without any food for us, for the potatoes he brought on his back the man took from him in payment for going to and from the woods.

The next day, Brother learned that just as he left the woods, the partner got frightened sitting there alone. Several times he wanted to flee, but he did not wish to leave the potatoes that someone might take. At last be got an idea. He would scatter the potatoes so that no one would discover them and take them. It did not enter his mind that by scattering the potatoes, he would not have them either. When he had done this, he took the cock under his arm and ran home. He would not give brother even half of the rooster, for he argued he had bought him, therefore, he was his.

Hurriedly, the Poles left our town. They seemed to be hard-pressed, for they had no time to stop and cause trouble. Hardly had they left town, when the Bolsheviki again made their appearance. There was no shooting by either side. It just seemed as if a badly frightened hare was being chased by a hard- pressing fox. The hare was too frightened to turn around and give battle. While the fox was too busy chasing to stop awhile and fight.

Towards the end of April the excitement, caused by the town changing from Polish dominance to Communistic dominance, wore off. The people settled down to the usual sluggish life of the small town. There was nothing to do; no work of any kind was to be had.

Brother Harry decided to go to the village without a partner. He also refused to take Brother and me along. He said it would be best for us to remain at home. The villagers were still perturbed over the recent evacuation of one army and the invasion of another. Both armies drafted the services of the peasants' horses. This was hard on the peasants who wanted to plough the fields and get them ready to plant. As a result of this hardship, the villagers were not in the best mood, and the refusal of the peasants to give their horses to the Bolsheviki was likely to start trouble. Therefore, the village was too hot a place for us yet.

At home we had nothing to do. We went around idle as did many others--adults and youths alike. The weather was extremely fair in Russia for that time of the year. Indeed, so warm were the days that the deep mud that were wont to abide in our town till late in May had dried, early in April in the balmy 1920 Spring. We no longer needed overcoats when we went outside for several hours; the sun was warm enough. And so all the idle of the town gathered about Michael, the American, in the market place and listened to his wonder stories.

Michael had come from America for his family just as the War between Russia and Germany broke out, as a result he had remained in Russia. He and his family had lived in a village. But when the Poles drove out all the Jews from the villages, he too, was one of the victims. Since our town was closest to the village in which he lived, he had moved there. Now that there was nothing to do he took great delight in relating stories of America.

Every day many people gathered about him and listened closely while he told us about strange things of the New World. We believed every word he uttered. One would have been thought a heretic had he questioned Michael's stories.

The first day as we, now unafraid of being dragged away to do some dirty work for the Poles, gathered in the market place, Michael, the American, who had, lived two years in New York treated us to an exhibition of his knowledge of the English language. This exhibition gave us the impression that the Americans were a laconic people. His English consisted of one or two words at a time. He assured us that everyone in America spoke exactly as he did:

"Hello," he explained meant in our tongue, "Good afternoon to you."

"Never mind," was equivalent to "Don't bother, everything is all right."

Then he started to expound the important part he took in "Nav York" life as he always thus pronounced the name of America's largest city. There, he said, he did not do mere manual work. No, he had a profession. With an outburst chest he proclaimed that he was a bluffer in America.

When this was off his chest, he waited a little for us to digest this word. He was about ready to fling another strange word in our ears, when someone in the audience irreverently asked, "What is a bluffer, Mr. Michael?"

The American was as astounded as the rest of the crowd at anybody having the nerve to question him, Had the crowd known who the audacious culprit was, it would have lynched him for interrupting such an important personage with silly questions. All that the American uttered should be taken for granted.

In a short time Mr. Michael became composed again, and to the surprise of us all he explained in our language that bluffer meant a banker.

Awed by this announcement, an old man close to Mr. Michael asked in a low respectful voice "Mr. Michael did you say a banker?"

"Sure,"

This curt answer astonished us even more.

"Is that a profession in America too?" asked a middle aged man, who prided himself on having been a clerk in the local bank under the Czar regime.

Mr. Michael respected no one, not even a former clerk of a bank.

"What a silly question?" The American now became disdainful.

"Sure, indicates that it is easy to become a banker in America. Why, I issued money with my name signed on it. Even the President was willing to accept my money. Most people in America do this very same thing."

America must be a very paradise I thought to myself. Just imagine to be able to issue money at will and everybody accepting it, even the President! This time the crowd was content to be satisfied with Mr. Michael's words. No one asked another question which might appear silly.

Now that Mr. Michael had regained his importance and everyone was eager to hear about the wonders of America, he launched into stories of New York. The happenings of these stories he himself had witnessed and therefore were the gospel truth:

"The first month that I had been in Nav York was walking with a friend of mine from work about seven o'clock in the evening. It was a day in June and the sun had not yet set. The two of us were talking about our families that we had left behind in Russia. All of a sudden we heard a cry for help.

Looking in the direction from which the call came we saw two boys fighting each other with their fists. The one that seemed to be getting the worse of it kept on calling for help. In a short time a crowd to witness the fight gathered. No one from the crowd interfered in the fighting, for there is a rule in America that when two fellows fight nobody should help either.

"About two or three minutes after we joined the crowd someone shouted, "The police!" Everybody, including the fighters, took to his heels and fled in all directions, we among them.

"We immediately forgot that incident and went into a restaurant to have supper. We ate a hearty meal; but, when we wanted to pay for the meal, we were astonished to find our wallets gone.

"The restaurant keeper told us, then, that the fight was staged to get a crowd. When the crowd is of a fair size, trained pickpockets mix with the people and lift as many valuables as they can from the by—standers.

"Thus the crooks work it in <u>Nav</u> <u>York</u>," our American friend concluded.

Every day Mr. Michael would dig up a story for us. The next day he related that three kinds of trains were running in New York. Most of his audience had never seen a train. It was said that about sixty miles away from our town a train was running. But the average townsman never went farther than twenty-five or thirty miles away from the town. Therefore, when a train was mentioned to us, we had to imagine it the best we could, for we had never had an opportunity to see a picture of a train.

I once overheard two old men talking about a train. They were walking along on the cobbled highway that ran through our town. I happened to walk in back of them, and as their conversation interested me, I followed them. They discussed the possibilities of a railroad being made on our highway.

One man said that the thirty feet-wide road would not be sufficiently wide for a train. While the other said that the highway would be just wide enough for a train. This discussion made my imagination enact before me a picture of a huge machine as a train. This train had no particular form or shape. Somehow I did not associate it with the automobile or airplane, both of which I had seen. No matter what its shape or appearance, it was nevertheless as huge as a monster.

When Mr. Michael mentioned the three trains in New York, I associated those trains with the huge formless thing of my imagination. But when the explanation stated that one kind of a train went underground, I was at a loss to account just how this thing could constantly plough through the underground--he never explained that extra tubes were made for these trains.

Another kind of train went on the ground he said. This was not as puzzling, for at least it had the solid ground as its road and there were no obstacles in its way as there would be for a train that went underground. At last he dumbfounded us all by announcing that another kind of train went up in the air. I could hardly imagine a huge thing being able to stay in the air with hundreds of people in it as Mr. Michael assured us it could. This was indeed a strange story. Otherwise we asked for no explanation.

These trains, he concluded, kept going back and forth every few minutes. The noise they caused was unbearable. Therefore, many people go crazy because of this terrific noise.

Mr. Michael told us a story each day. He kept track carefully of what he had related and never made the error of repeating a story. He, furthermore, presented his tales unhesitatingly. He talked of them as if they were occurring before him at the time of the telling. Before one story, only, he hesitated, looked around and asked the crowd if there were any female listeners in the audience. When he was assured that just males were around him, he regained his composure and began his tale.

"In Nav York a man leaves for work at seven o'clock in the morning. While he slaves and sweats in dingy, dirty shops to earn a miserable living, his wife at home takes it easy. She sleeps till about eleven o'clock. When she is at last awakened by the hungry child, she gets up and quiets the young one with a bottle of milk. After the woman eats her late breakfast, which also serves as lunch, she goes out on the stoop to gossip with the neighbors."

"When the man, at last, completes his hard day's work and returns home about seven o'clock at night, he is greeted by a dirty home. "Oh! Charles," breaks down the wife as her husband makes his entrance, "baby has been unusually bad today. All day long, I kept him in my arms to keep him from crying. As a result, I could not clean up. Here, hold the baby while I run down to the delicatessen. What will you have for dinner, corn beef or bologna?"

"The tired man submissively eats the unpalatable, indigestible, cold meal. When the dinner is finished, the wife suggests that they take a walk and cool off a little in the open air."

"This sounds not so bad. The man feels that he needs some fresh air after such an un-refreshing meal. But before he has spent half an hour outside, he is sorry that he left the house, for besides pushing the baby in the carriage, he is additionally weighted down by the burden of his wife hanging on his arm."

"Thus the men in Nav York," concluded the American philosophically, "day in and day out slave either at the shops or in their homes."

CHAPTER XIV
CULTURE

By May the first, the Bolsheviki had established themselves to stay. Also, they did not let this great holiday pass without a celebration. A big band played the Internationalé and the other Communistic strains. The whole town turned out to listen to silver tongued orators in the market place. We could not help being happy when we heard the promises to the Proletariat. Everyone wore a happy expression on his face and proudly displayed the bit of red on his person to show his patriotism.

When the speeches ended, we children were lined up. For the first time in many years, such a delicacy as candy was distributed to us. At the sight of it we were overjoyed and began to think that the promises were being fulfilled already. But when food--a thing which was to us emaciated children even of more importance than candy--was not distributed to us that day, our enthusiasm began to cool off. When night came we were tired of the day's celebrations on an empty stomach, and were greatly disappointed.

The town's disappointment soon was gone. Under an able young man from Odessa, literary clubs were formed. The youths of the town flocked to these clubs. Many different books were furnished as free reading material. Lecturers, to whom everyone could listen without paying for admission, were brought to town.

Before and after the lectures the audience sang the Internationalé. The strains of this song greatly thrilled us small children, loitering outside of the auditorium. Upon hearing the song we immediately hushed our chatter and silently, thoughtfully listened to the beautiful tune and the inspiring words.

Not always did the youth go to the literary clubs just to read. They more often gathered to discuss different topics of interest. We, the younger children, who were barred from these clubs, because of our immaturity stood on the outside and, through the open windows, watched the proceedings within. The enthusiastic boys and girls alertly discussed important matters. Now their faces were bright, now earnest and thoughtful. Only by watching their sensitive, changing features could we tell whether the thing under discussion was important or whether one or another had presented his point well. Three young people had hungered for intellectual work for years, and now that they had the opportunity to receive some culture, they pounced upon it like hungry wolves and still could not satisfy their craving.

Once a week this enthusiastic group gathered to sing. On these nights, we, the younger comrades, did not forget to take up our posts outside of the clubs to listen to the beautiful strains. When singing the various hymns--the most prominent of which were the Marseillaise and the Internationalé, the boys and girls become inspired. They were enthralled by these hymns and they put in them their whole hearts as well as hearty lungs. Outside we listened with great awe to the songs that promised so much to the long downtrodden Proletariat.

As the summer approached, these young people began to present plays for the enjoyment of the whole public. Under the guidance of the learned young man from Odessa, the boys and girls performed wonders. The older people said that the weekly plays were much better than plays they had seen presented by so-called professionals. These weekly theatrical performances were free to the public. The Proletariat, however, got first choice of seats. Therefore, I occupied a front seat.

The great singer, who, while in our town, ushered in the war, was also brought to entertain the Proletariat. Again the big synagogue was reserved for this occasion. This time our entire family received tickets for the great treat, and I sat well towards the front instead of in a cramped hidden position under a low bench. The Internationalé was sung at the beginning and at the end of the concert.

CHAPTER XV
THE TOBACCO FIELDS

Concerts and theaters were food for the mind. But being human, we needed food for the body also. This food was now as hard to get as was food for the mind before the war.

Brother Harry could no longer find work in the village. The little clothes the peasants had, had been made over. New material for new clothes could not be obtained for any price; therefore, Harry was out of work. He, nevertheless, visited the village weekly, hoping that some work would turn up, but almost always returned disappointed.

When the Bolsheviki returned, they immediately announced that males twenty-one years of age or over could obtain some of the nobles' lands that were being distributed. Many men applied for and received permission to cultivate tracts of land, which were larger than they needed for the growing of vegetables for their own consumption. For several weeks these men were at a loss to know what to do with the excess acreage. Finally, having discovered that there was great demand for tobacco, they decided to plant tobacco in the remaining fields.

The people who had gotten the land somehow procured capital to hire boys and girls to work the fields. Although the day's earnings of a tobacco laborer were just enough for the purchase of a pound of black bread, numerous boys and girls turned out to work on these fields.

Sister, Brother Sam, and I sought employment there. The employer looked us over and decided that he could use Sister and Brother but not me. He said I was too small to work on tobacco fields. Upon hearing this, I ran home crying and complaining to Mother that the man refused to employ me. I insisted that she come with me to the man and convince him that I would be as useful as an adult.

At last Mother consented to go with me to the employer. She told him how much the earnings of the three of us would mean to the family. She said that what I would earn would mean food for me at least, whereas if I was refused a job, the earnings of Sister and Brother would not be sufficient to feed us all. The man was moody and not moved by this. Yet he maintained that the season would soon be over and he needed strong people to do quick planting. When Mother told him to pay me less than the regular wage, he agreed to employ me only with the condition that I do the same amount of work as any other worker. And so at the age of thirteen, I found myself taking an adult's job.

At seven o'clock the next morning, the three of us, together with seven others piled into a wagon drawn by a single horse. After about a five-mile ride from the town, we reached the field.

At this early hour, the sun was already burning fiercely over the tobacco fields on which we were to work. There was not a single place in those vast fields that escaped the heat. The fields were ideally situated for the growing of tobacco, but they were not so inviting to those about to engage in a day of labor on them.

As soon as we reached the plantation, each one was assigned a row for planting. I was on an outside row, so that the foreman, I presume, could keep an eye on me. Each worker was given a pointed stick with which to bore a hole in the ground for the planting of the tobacco, and also was provided with a small basket full of tobacco plants. This basket of plants was just enough for one row of the field, I was instructed.

We were then told to start working. Under a scorching sun I stooped over and worked feverishly to keep up with the other planters. With one hand I bored a hole; and even as I pulled the stick out of the soil, a plant was ready in the other hand to be set into the hole and made firm in the soil. Down the field I crawled, working as fast as my strength would allow. From the corner of my eye, I watched her working on the row next to me. I was told that she was the fastest on the field, and I, a novice at this work, had to compete with her. Perspiration rolled down my forehead and into my eyes. These salty drops made my eyes smart, and consequently my work became slower. With my dirty hands, I wiped the perspiration away and began working even more vigorously. My neighbor was well in front of me now, and I wondered how to catch up to her. The harder I worked, the farther back I found myself. Once, when the foreman departed for a while, the girl next to me, who had seen my plight, immediately switched to my row and started planting to help me. Before the man returned our two rows were even, and now she purposely slackened in her work that I might keep up with her. I was only a yard behind her when she finished the planting of her row, and this pleased the foreman greatly.

My benefactor was now seeing to it that I should be next to her. She constantly advised me how to get along faster in the planting. "Bore several holes at one at the same time, and then set in the plants. You'll find this much quicker." these are the words she said.

I was eager to do so and found that I benefited by her helpful suggestions. Little by little the strain of trying to keep up with the adult workers became less. The unaccustomed stooping for a long period of time caused terrible pains in my back at first. For the first two hours, these pains were almost unbearable. My muscles, however, soon became numb to the pain while I was stooping; and as my thoughts were 'wholly taken up with my task, I soon was unaware of the pangs in my back.

Then the hour for lunch arrived. The sudden straightening of my body resulted in terrible agonies. It seemed as if several thousand fine-pointed needles had just been injected into my back. Although this pain lasted for only two minutes, nevertheless, it was the most severe that I had ever experienced.

When I had joined my Sister and Brother we unwrapped the half-pound of mush made of corn maize that Mother had given us. The cold mush alone served as our lunch. We could not even procure any water to quench our thirst. Our soiled hands did not lessen our appetites. After we had finished the scanty meal we even licked our fingers to avoid wasting any of the small bits that stuck to our dirty hands.

When the half hour allowed for lunch was over, we again returned to the backbreaking job. We were joyful because we were employed and knew that at night we would get paid. This assured us of bread or mush for the next day. I rejoiced ever more when the boss informed me at the end of the day that I might return to work the next day. These, indeed, were good tidings to me.

After each one received the day's pay, the boss ordered us to take our seats in the wagon for the return. The wagon was too small for all of us to sit inside. Therefore, it was filled with straw, and we seated ourselves on the sides of the wagon, our feet hanging out on the outside. I procured a similar seat on the back of the wagon when the sides could no longer hold any passengers.

Meanwhile large clouds began to form in the sky. A storm was imminent. To avoid the possible storm, the boss whipped the horse into a fast trot. The horse, mad with the stings of the biting whip, ran wildly to one side and over into a deep pigs' pool. The load was much too heavy for a single horse to pull out of this hole. Under the merciless beating of the man, the animal tugged at the wagon wheels this way and that way. At last the load began to move. The front wheels were about out of the ditch when the horse slipped, the wagon upset, and we all fell into the muddy water.

"Say, do you want to remain there?" I heard several girls teasing me as they pulled me out of the mud.

I regained my senses, they continued, "You were on the bottom of this hole and, therefore, thoroughly covered with mud. We all had scrambled to our feet and had taken our seats again in the wagon when Rose, your new sweetheart, cried out that you were missing."

Rose, beside whom I had worked the whole day, started wiping away the mud from my face, eyes, and mouth. Then she removed my wet clothing and loaned me one of her petticoats. In this array she brought me home to my astonished Mother.

The next day I was again working under the blazing sun. I did not dare stay home a day for fear of losing my job.

Through the whole summer, the three of us worked on the tobacco plantations. When the planting season was over, we watered the small plants. Then we hoed them again and again. Early in the fall, we were at hand to gather the tobacco leaves off the fields.

Even when the tobacco was off the fields, we still found employment. The green leaves had to be packed together and covered with hay. When the tobacco leaves remained so for a week the deep green shade turned to a beautiful yellow gold.

After going through the above process, the tobacco was strung and dried. In dingy dark attics, the three of us, together with several others, performed the difficult task of stringing tobacco leaves. The stringing was first done on large, pointed, two- edged shaped needle. From thence the leaves were transferred to a long cord. A regular-sized cord of twenty feet had three full—packed needles of tobacco leaves. These cords were stretched in large, lofty barns. Then the leaves were carefully separated so that no two leaves stuck together. This was the drying process.

We, however, did only the stringing. The drying was done by others. After three weeks of constant work with the long sword-like needle, we were experts in this work. We no longer feared that the big steel point would go into our finger at the same time that it went through the tobacco leaf, as happened several times in our first few days work on it. Now we could do the work quickly and efficiently even with our eyes closed. Working the whole day in this automatic way made machines out of us and we worked as fast as machines. Finally we refused to work by the day as a basis for pay. We demanded and got payment for the number of needles strung. This helped us earn two kopecks more a day. Thus we worked away on a dark and cloudy day in September of 1920, when Mother rushed in anxious with tears in her eyes and exclaimed:

"Stop working, my children, Father has sent us money from America!"

At last the long-looked-for relief had arrived!

****

PART 2
ISADORE'S LEADERSHIP AWARD
FROM B'NAI B'RITH

Isadore Weiss gave the following speech to the East Windsor B'nai B'rith Lodge where Isadore received a leadership award for his service as President. B'nai B'rith has at least half a million members in over fifty countries and provides charity and support for the Jewish people and the community at large.

Figure 1 Isadore Weiss receiving a leadership award from B'nai B'rith

Isadore's Comments Made at the B'nai B'rith Awards Presentation.

WHAT JUDAISM MEANS TO ME BY ISADORE WEISS

I was born a Jew. As a Jewish child in Russia Judaism meant to me physical and mental pain. The hordes led by Deniken, Kolchak, or Petlura swooped down like locusts on the Jewish population. They sacked our houses, they burned our synagogues, they violated our women, and massacred those unfortunate Jews who did not find a safe hiding place. Those of us who escaped being massacred were continually hunted like animals while we suffered from hunger, from cold, from disease, and from constant fear of the beasts in the shape of man. But despite all this misery, despite all this suffering, despite all this fear, there were the precious moments of attending services with the remnant of the Russian Jewry. There were the precious moments when, on the Sabbath, the spirit of God seemed present in the house when Mother lit the candles, when the Kiddush was chanted. There were the Simchas Torah celebrations when we exalted in the possession of the Torah and its many treasures. There were the sessions around the table with the Rabbis, listening to the wisdom that was read from the Talmud.

Later as a young man in the United States, Judaism meant to me subtle exclusions from professions in which I wanted to engage. I look to the time when I graduated from high school. I had a talk with the Dean of the University to which I sought admission. I was asked for a list of professions in which I want to engage. I listed medicine, chemical engineering, and law.

The Dean looked at me and said: "Young man, you will have difficulty getting into a medical school, you will have difficulty finding a position as an engineer and you will have difficulty finding a legal position with a big corporation. My advice to you is to study accounting. Should you have difficulty finding a position as an accountant, your accounting background will be helpful to you in any business endeavor that you might engage in."

I studied accounting. But during this period, too, I was sustained by the Jewishness around me at home and by my daily visits to the Synagogue to say

Kaddish for my deceased father, which again brought me into contact with the rich Jewish Heritage which I cherish so.

Now Judaism means to me the identification with a people that has a culture dating back thousands of years. In my mind I am exalted at the thought that this Jewish culture has been a catalyst in the production of such great minds as those possessed by Ehrlich, Schick, Einstein, Salk, and others. I don't have to feel apologetic for being a Jew. My inward pride inspires me to be a Jew and to guide my offspring in the ways of Jewishness.

Figure 2 The extended family of Isadore Weiss 1994

Top Row – Left to Right, Nancy Weiss-Meyer, Marc Weiss, Michael Gottesman, Lewis Meixler, Deborah Meixler, Andrew Zwerin, Steven Spierer, Barry Weiss, Michael Meixler, Alan Zwerin, Mona Gottesman, Jerry Gottesman, Miriam Zwerin and David Zwerin.

Middle Row – Left to Right, Dani Gottesman, Marci Meixler, Sylvia Weiss, Carol Weiss, Amy Zwerin, and Sylvia's sister Gloria Spierer.

Front Row – Left to Right, Melanie Spierer, Joe Spierer, Amy Weiss-Meyer on lap, Matthew Weiss and Michele Weiss.

Figure 3 Mr. and Mrs. Sylvia Weiss 1980s

Part 3
Introduction to Sylvia Weiss
by Dr. Eamon P. Doherty

Isadore and Sylvia Weiss were married for 56 years. I had the pleasure of meeting Sylvia and her daughter, Deborah in September of 2008 when we began the process of composing this book. Mrs. Weiss looks 15-20 years younger than her real age, and she had four wonderful children, nine grandchildren, and ten great grandchildren. Mrs. Weiss was born and raised in America and has seen a great many changes in her lifetime. Her life spans such tragedies as WWI, the Depression, WWII, the Holocaust and the use of an atomic bomb in Japan. But she has also seen remarkable things such as man landing on the moon and a wonderful prosperous life for all her children, grandchildren and great grandchildren. Mrs. Weiss' viewpoints and experiences are very important because they bridge the ways of life from the beginning of the twentieth century to the beginning of the twenty-first century.

SYLVIA WEISS

A stay-at-home-mother, Sylvia says her greatest achievement was to raise four fine and loving children. She boasts nine grandchildren and ten great grand children. Among other interests, Sylvia volunteered in PTA, Girl and Boy Scouting, Hadassah, and League of Women Voters. She wrote East Windsor N.J.'s first "Know Your Town" publication. She also authored a cookbook for Hadassah as a fundraiser.

Sylvia initiated and developed East Windsor's Senior Citizen Program in the early 1970's and it served as a model for other New Jersey communities. As the program evolved, she wrote a weekly column for the Windsor-Hights Herald. That ultimately led to elected office as a councilwoman. She also served as a Director on the Board of Elderhostel. East Windsor's Mayor has established an annual event at which a senior citizen receives a plaque named, "The Sylvia Weiss Volunteer Award"

Figure 4 Sylvia Weiss 2008

ISADORE WEISS
BY SYLVIA WEISS

For Isadore the United States was truly the Promised Land. He was passionate in his belief that only in America could one prosper and grow by honest ambition, hard work, and modest living. That was the way he lived. His dreams were realized and his progeny followed, each generation surpassing the one before.

His introduction to this country was not easy. He arrived here at the age of fourteen. Because he did not know English, the teacher wanted to place him in the first grade, but he was too big to fit in the chair beneath the desk. So, they moved him to a higher grade. Because he excelled, he was able to complete Grade School and High School by the age of 18. He wrote the book "Looking Back" when he had been in this country only six years. While attending grade school, immediately upon coming to this country, he went to work with his father, who had established a dry cleaning-tailor shop. Despite Isadore's lack of English, he was charged with picking up and delivering clothing walking or using public transportation. His father, a hard-working man, offered only abuse when Isadore could not find the customer's house from which to pick up and deliver. Of course, his father did not have it easy either. He had labored in sweatshops in America through the period of World War I, living in deprivation, in order to send money home to Europe before he set up his own humble business. His health suffered and he died suddenly, less than two years after his family had joined him.

Upon their father's death, the family split. The eldest four adult children kept the modest house and business. Isadore and his brother Sam, together with their mother, bought another small row house in the East End of Pittsburgh. With the advice and generosity of his Uncle Hyman, who gave them an old pressing machine, converted the living room into a dry cleaning-tailoring shop.

Two years older than Isadore, Sam was tormented by classmates. He had never been an apt student and had difficulty with the new language. He hated school and dropped out as soon as the law allowed. Sam had learned tailoring as an apprentice to his grandfather; so he worked the shop through the day. Isadore put in an equal number of hours after school. He continued to knock on doors after school hours, picking up and delivering by foot, and also operated the pressing machine. Their mother, who never learned English, was happy to keep the house for the boys.

Despite the heavy workload, Isadore excelled in high school, earning highest honors when he graduated. He was offered a 4-year scholarship at the University of Pittsburgh and for a day, dreamed of being a doctor.

However, he followed the advice of his unlettered Uncle Hyman. Hyman thought it would be too difficult to withstand the jibes of Sam who was openly envious, claiming Isadore was not putting in his fair share of time in the shop. Additionally, Hyman pointed out that the boys were beginning to establish themselves with promise of better things to come. What good was a degree, he reasoned? Isadore turned the scholarship down.

An Americanized, and more knowledgeable cousin, learned of it and phoned, urging Isadore to reconsider, but it was too late. The scholarship had already been passed to a second student. The teacher, who had championed the original scholarship, sought to obtain another one. He was successful only in that the second scholarship was limited to the School of Business Administration at the University. Isadore continued to work in the shop while he earned a degree in accounting.

By the time he graduated, our country was deep in depression. Accounting firms were not hiring Jews and certainly not those with a foreign accent. Undaunted, Isadore started to pursue a private practice with some success, but it was a continuation of working late hours and weekends to accommodate his clients. And it was difficult to make a living; so he pursued a career in U.S. Civil Service, progressing through three separate federal agencies until retirement.

By this time we were already married and had our first child. Together we decided if we were to have a normal life as a family, we would all be better off if he entered civil service with the Federal Government. It was the right decision. He progressed, advancing through the system until his retirement in 1976.

Although there were periods when his work required travel away from home, Isadore managed to volunteer in the schools, as well as civically, in the several different communities where we lived. He was a devoted father of four, and lived to enjoy grand and great grand children.

Isadore and I were married soon after he graduated from Pitt and he experienced much joy in our four children as well as grandchildren and great grandchildren. He was happy in his ability to support each of them in attaining their education without hardship.

Throughout his life, Isadore was animated by two ideas. One was his respect for the value of education. He was dedicated to providing it for each of his children and grandchildren, always living modestly toward that end. The second was his never-failing appreciation of our country, its freedom and its "golden opportunities."

His appreciation of our country's promise never faded.

Figure 5 Isadore and Sylvia Weiss wedding photo

Sylvia in front row center, Isadore behind, Isadore's mother, Mirrel on Sylvia's left and Sylvia's mother Lily Dichner on right.   Sylvia's father, Jacob Dichner is at the end of the rear row on the right.

PART 4
THE ISADORE WEISS AUDIO TAPES
BY DR. EAMON DOHERTY

HIGHLIGHTS FROM THE TAPES

Mel Weiss, Isadore's nephew recorded the memoirs of Isadore Weiss in a set of audio tapes in 1989. They reveal that Isadore's father, Meyer Nissan Weissman was the president of one of the synagogue's in Minkovitz and was concerned about people not being able to purchase homes and have a place to live. Meyer therefore co-signed many loans for them to purchase homes. The audio tapes and Yizkor books both state that there was little work in Minkovitz, and what was available was agricultural, with the result that many people could not pay their loans and defaulted. Meyer Weissman was therefore responsible for their payments and did not have enough income to pay. He therefore went to America to earn money to send back to repay all this debt.

EMIGRATION TO THE USA

Isadore recalled in the tapes that his grandfather, Mr. Lazaravitch, went from the Ukraine to Romania back in the 1800s. There was a river between the Ukraine and Romania and many people were often smuggled out that way. Minkovitz was approximately 30 miles from the part of the river where people crossed. Mr. Lazaravitch married a woman in Romania and then ended up in the USA. He had many single male relatives in the Ukraine and his wife had many single female relatives. Mr. Lazaravitch then played matchmaker and helped arrange marriages between these men and women, which brought some relatives and friends to America.

Those in the United States would start working and provide tickets for passage for other people in Romania or the Ukraine to go to the United States or for some to go back and visit. A visiting relative would sometimes convince other relatives to go back with them to the United States. Harry, Isadore's older brother, smuggled himself out of the Ukraine and earned some money. Once Harry saved up enough he smuggled himself back over the border to the Ukraine, and then visited his brother Sam, Isadore, his mother, and their sister Sylvia [not to be confused with Isadore's wife, also Sylvia].

Isadore, Sam, Harry, their mom, and Sylvia lived in a nice stone house with two floors and a tin roof until they left when Isadore was about 12 years old. Most people had very modest houses many of which had roofs made of organic material such as bundled grasses and dirt floors. Isadore's family had worthy possessions, such as pinfeather pillows, candlesticks, and other household goods. The pillows had been laboriously made by the whole family by stripping the down from goose feathers over many winters, and were a family treasure. Some of these pillows are still in the Weiss family, as a family heirloom. When they left the Ukraine, they had to do it covertly as if they were moving to a new house in a village nearby. Even though the Russians and Ukrainians treated the Jewish population badly at times, they did not want the Jews to leave the country.

Isadore recalls in the audio tapes how Harry arranged with some smugglers ahead of time to have the family smuggled out. A system of tokens, hidden money, and various contacts along the route in Romania and the Ukraine were used because the smugglers were known to be corrupt and betrayed one another or their clients. Here how Isadore said the system worked. Once they were smuggled out, Harry would tell the smuggler to bring an object, such as a candlestick to a trusted contact, Mr. X in the destination village in Romania. Mr. X would then give the smuggler a map that revealed where the money was hidden. This was done so that Harry and the family would be assured of getting smuggled out and not just robbed, betrayed, and arrested.

THE FIRST ATTEMPT TO GO TO AMERICA

In the tapes, Isadore recalls their attempts to leave Minkovitz. Harry had arranged with the smugglers to get the family out of the Ukraine. They waited until certain border guards were working, the river was low, the moonlight was minimal and other conditions for escape were perfect. Then they prepared to move in with two carts of household items. Harry went on to arrange things but while in the village waiting, the Bolsheviks arrested Sylvia, Isadore, his mother, and Sam and put them all in jail in a basement. The basement had no partition and Isadore and his brothers and mother and sister were held there together with six men. The Bolsheviks sent back the two carts of items. There were no sanitary conditions. There was one guard and an outhouse, and no food the first day. The guard ate peaches in front of Isadore and spat the pits at him. Louie Walters, a family friend, brought Isadore's family food once a day while they were in jail for five days. Harry then was able to meet with a high ranking communist who was a friend of his father who arranged their release from jail. They all went home 30 miles barefoot in the hot summer. The mayor vouched they lived there.

THE SECOND ATTEMPT TO GO TO AMERICA

The family was awaiting trial and recalled how terrible the experience was, and they resolved that they were not going to attempt that again. However, when they got the two carts of silver candelabras, pillows, jewelry, a gold watch, and the rest of their possessions back, they again contacted the smuggler and tried again with two new carts.

Once they got across the river into Romania, the smugglers were given an item from the wagon that served as a token with which they could redeem their fee with a pre-selected person in one of the local villages. In Romania, the guide took them to a house with a large outdoor potato cellar. Because the roads were guarded, they were forced to remain there for approximately three days with only a little stale bread and water for subsistence. Then they walked and slept on the fields as they continued their journey. Once they moved from the fields to the roads, they encountered some Romanian soldiers with whom they shared no common language. The soldiers seemed to be discussing if they should arrest these people and take them to the Russian border. At that moment Harry dropped a paper bank note, which the Romanian soldiers picked up. The soldiers lost interest in these travelers and everyone continued on their previous paths. The tapes continue with their travels to the United States

Isadore moved to Pittsburgh, Pennsylvania at about age 12, together with Sam, Isadore's mother, and his sister, with the help of HIAS [Hebrew Immigrant Aid Society]. Isadore learned English and helped with his father's business. Shortly after, his father died and was buried in the Pittsburgh area. Sam and Isadore worked the family dry cleaning and tailoring business from their living room while their mother took care of the house. Isadore eventually secured a college scholarship, graduated business school with honors, and worked for the Department of Corrections and then various other government agencies. Sam worked the dry cleaning and tailoring business until he retired. Upon retiring, he sold it to two young men who were not Jewish according to the audiotapes. Sam was married when he was young and his picture can be seen in the photos.

THE WORK OF HIAS

Mrs. Weiss told me that the Hebrew Immigration Aid Society [HIAS], is an organization that assists many Jewish people who relocate to a new country. They help them with training, clothes, finding a place to live, and sometimes getting started in business. Meyer Weiss (Weissman), set up a tailoring and dry cleaning business there because of the assistance he received from HIAS. Mrs. Weiss continues to support this organization and its charity to the needy.

According to the Yizkor book for Minkovitz, Yiddish was the spoken language of the Ukrainian Jewish community. The Jewish community spoke little or no Russian. Yiddish is related to 16th century German, somewhat similar to Pennsylvania Dutch as the Amish speak it. A person, who has a working knowledge of German, can often get the gist of what is said in a Yiddish conversation.

In an interview with Mrs. Weiss on October 25, 2008, she remarked that Isadore had a heavy Yiddish accent and felt the effects of anti-Semitism in the United States. However, he did not let that discourage him. Isadore took a civil service test, did well, and then pursued a career in the United States Civil Service, beginning with the Bureau of Prisons at the Penitentiary in Lewisburg, Pennsylvania. From the materials provided by his family, it appears his intellect, sense of justice, and compassion, provided the Penitentiary with someone who worked hard to help the prison run well.

THE SALAD OIL KING

Years later, Isadore was an investigator for the Department of Commerce. Anthony De Angelis, known in the press as "The Salad Oil King," was defrauding the government and the banks with exports of salad oil diluted with water. It is well known that oil and water do not mix. The water was heavier and sank while the salad oil rose to the top of the tanks, which served to deceive those evaluating the amount of salad oil. Having reviewed the De Angelis account books, Isadore determined there could not be the amount of oil as claimed. He climbed to the top of the tanks to verify his findings. Isadore found that the oil was only a few feet deep and the rest of the tank was filled with water. Isadore said in the audiotapes that two workmen that he believed were involved in the scam, tried to push him into the tank but he was able to foil their efforts. Unfortunately there were no witnesses to this incident. Isadore did not budge in the face of danger. Isadore claimed that a key person in the "Salad Oil Scam" tried to bribe him and threatened to harm his family. Isadore did not take the bribe and was not deterred by the threat. Isadore also said on the tapes that he found one of Mr. De Angelis' business associates in Virginia and went to see him. The associate said that the scam was ingenious because there were a series of pipes underground that allowed the contents of one tank be moved to the others, similar to a shell game. Isadore's relentless investigation of all aspects of the case from financial record examinations to the implementation of the scam, helped break the case and put the criminals behind bars. Ironically, De Angelis was put in the Lewisburg, Pennsylvania Federal Penitentiary where Isadore previously worked.

The details of this scam, are available on the Internet by searching Anthony "Tino" De Angelis and his company, *"Allied Crude Vegetable Oil Refining Corporation."*

The case that Isadore helped break was a major fraud that involved over 150 million dollars, American Express, and numerous banks. Norman C. Miller, the Pulitzer Prize winning journalist for the Wall Street Journal covered the story. Miller wrote "The Salad Oil King", which can still be found for sale on the Amazon Book website.

PART 5 ISADORE WEISS' FAMILY PHOTOS AND IMMIGRATION DOCUMENTS

The following section includes photos, background information on Isadore's brothers, sister, mother, and father, Meyer Nissan Weissman and documents related to their immigration to the United States. Various names appear for the same person in the documents. When one of Isadore's brothers entered the U. S. Army, his surname was shortened from Weissman to Weiss, which was adopted by the rest of the family. At the end of his Army service, he received his U. S. citizenship. Jewish people, especially those from Eastern Europe, often have an American name, a Hebrew name, and a Yiddish name. Some of the documents in this chapter, such as in the immigration papers, show that Isadore Weiss was originally Itsik Vaisman. Itsik was changed to Isadore at someone's advice to be more American. Vaisman was mostly likely recorded as Weissman, because the V is pronounced as a W, and the immigration authorities probably used this spelling.

Isadore Weiss Family Tree

The family tree below shows the siblings of Isadore Weiss, his ancestors, and his direct descendents. A more complete family tree is available on the WEB site www.isadoreweiss.com.

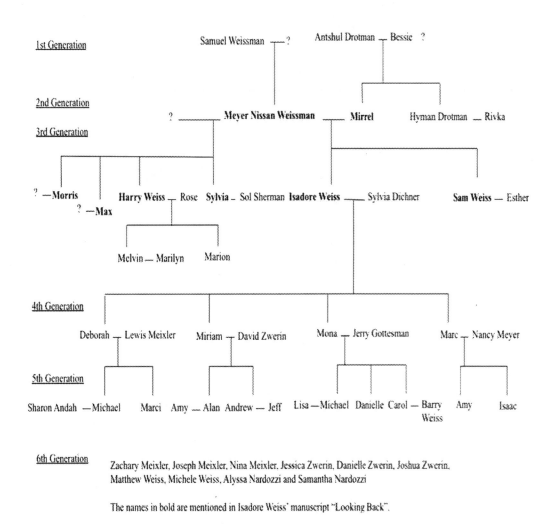

Figure 6 Isadore Weiss family tree

PHOTOS OF WEISS FAMILY MEMBERS

Figure 7 Isadore's Mother, Mirrel, brother Sam and Isadore in the U. S.

Figure 8 Harry Weiss

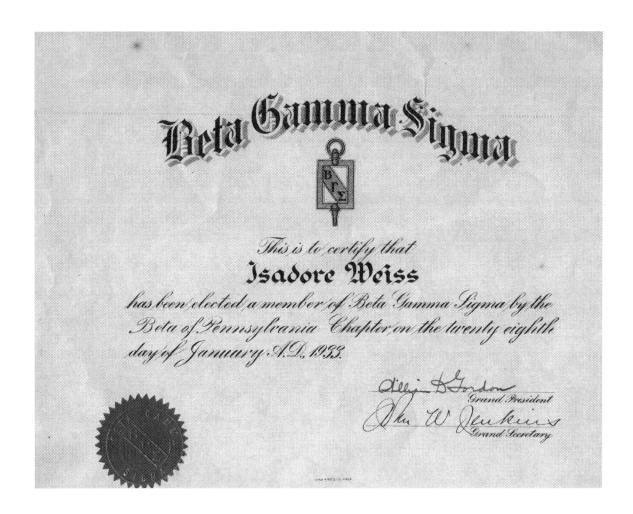

Figure 9 University of Pittsburgh National Honor Society Certificate

Figure 10   University of Pittsburgh graduation photo of Isadore Weiss

Figure 11 Isadore's father, Meyer Nissan Weissman.[1]

---

[1]   The name was later shortened to Weiss

Figure 12 Isadore Weiss as a young adult

IMMIGRATION INFORMATION AND DOCUMENTS

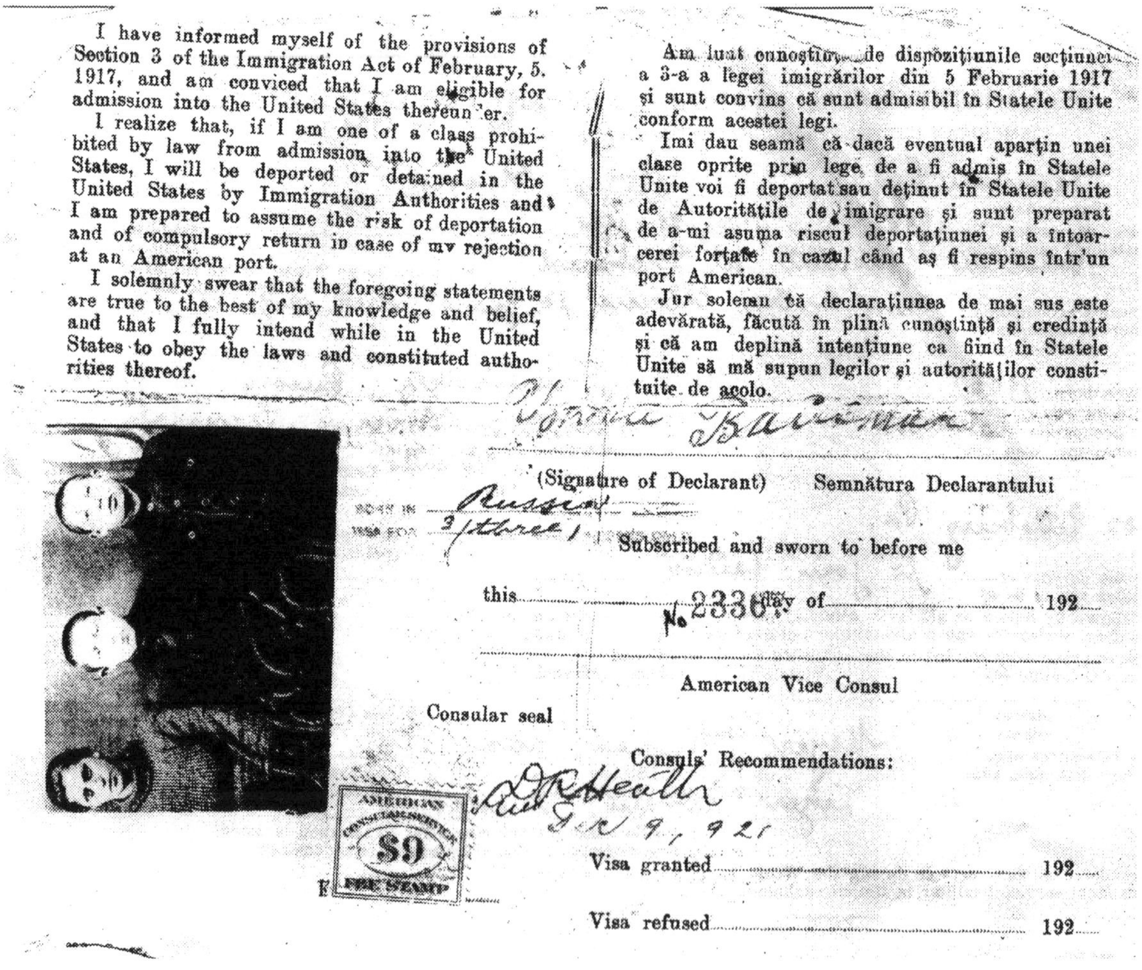

I have informed myself of the provisions of Section 3 of the Immigration Act of February, 5. 1917, and am convinced that I am eligible for admission into the United States thereunder.

I realize that, if I am one of a class prohibited by law from admission into the United States, I will be deported or detained in the United States by Immigration Authorities and I am prepared to assume the risk of deportation and of compulsory return in case of my rejection at an American port.

I solemnly swear that the foregoing statements are true to the best of my knowledge and belief, and that I fully intend while in the United States to obey the laws and constituted authorities thereof.

Am luat cunoştinţă de dispoziţiunile secţiunei a 3-a a legei imigrărilor din 5 Februarie 1917 şi sunt convins că sunt admisibil în Statele Unite conform acestei legi.

Imi dau seamă că dacă eventual aparţin unei clase oprite prin lege, de a fi admis în Statele Unite voi fi deportat sau deţinut în Statele Unite de Autorităţile de imigrare şi sunt preparat de a-mi asuma riscul deportaţiunei şi a intoarcerei forţate în cazul când aş fi respins într'un port American.

Jur solemn că declaraţiunea de mai sus este adevărată, făcută în plină cunoştinţă şi credinţă şi că am deplină intenţiune ca fiind în Statele Unite să mă supun legilor şi autorităţilor constituite de acolo.

(Signature of Declarant)   Semnătura Declarantului

Subscribed and sworn to before me

this _____ day of _____ 192___

American Vice Consul

Consular seal

Consuls' Recommendations:

Visa granted _____ 192___

Visa refused _____ 192___

Figure 13 Visa application for Sylvia, Isadore, and Sam

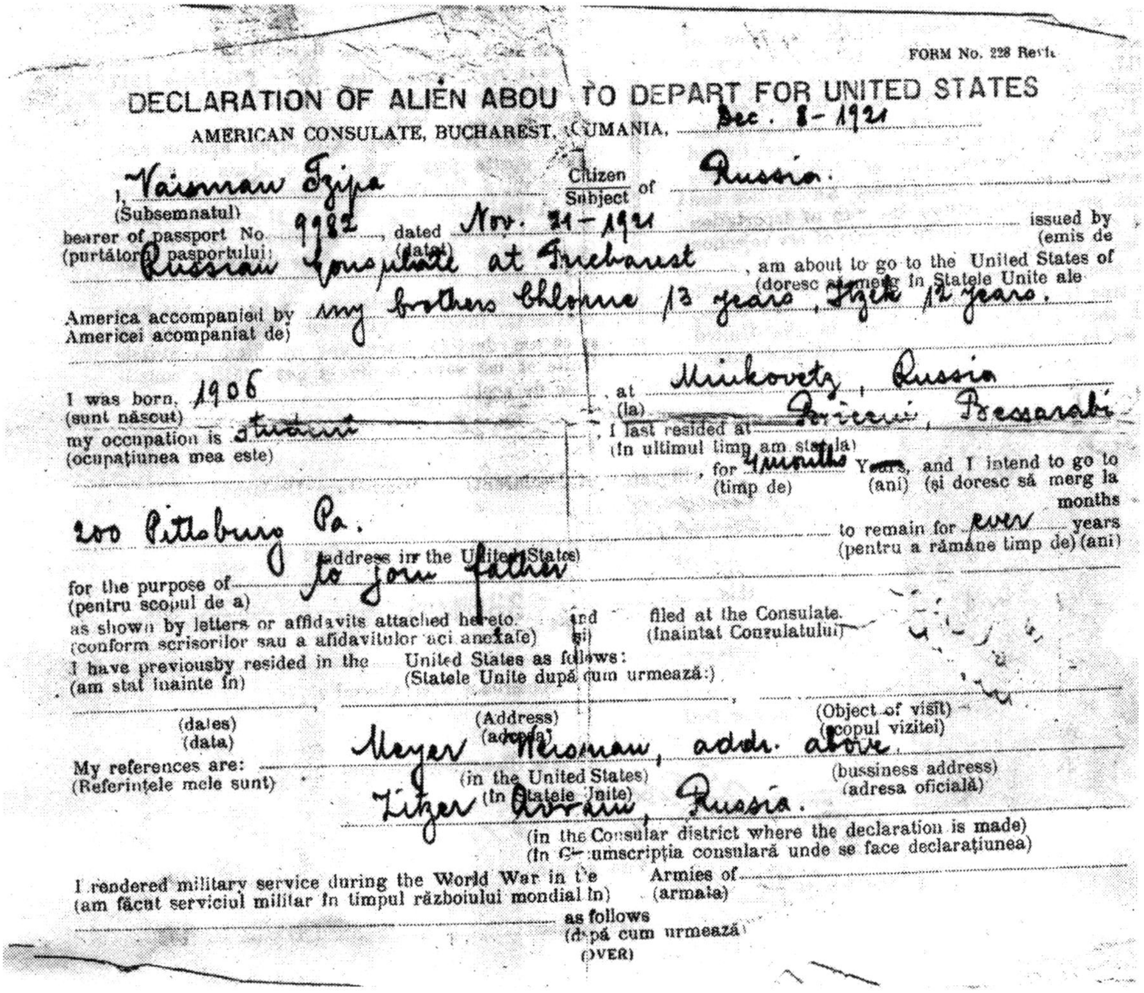

Figure 14 Sylvia's (Tsipe) immigration papers also listing Sam (Shlomo) and Isadore (Itzik).

[Note surname listed as Vaisman]

THE ORBITA

The ship that Isadore came to America on in 1921 was the Orbita. It was built by Harland and Wolf of Belfast, Ireland for the Royal Mail Steam Packet Co. Its capacity was 15,486 gross tons. It was launched in 1915 and was immediately requisitioned by the Royal Navy and used as a troopship in WW I, before she could be delivered. The maiden commercial voyage was September 26, 1919 from Liverpool, England to Rio de Janeiro. She was requisitioned again for service in World War II. She continued in commercial service after WW II and was finally sold for scrap in 1950.

Figure 15 1918 photo of the Orbita from the Ellis Island web site [2].

[2]   http://www.ellisisland.org/search/shipImage.asp?MID=18912350460180839616&pID=10 0007050265&

RMSP "ORBITA" (TRIPLE SCREW—15486 TONS) CABIN CLASS SERVICE TO NEW YORK

Figure 16 Another image of the Orbita from a contemporary postcard

IMMIGRATION RECORDS

STATES IMMIGRATION OFFICER AT PORT OF ARRIVAL

States, or a port of another insular possession, in whatsoever class they travel, MUST be fully listed and the master or commanding officer of each vessel carrying such passengers must upon arrival deliver Lists ther
STEERAGE PASSENGERS ONLY

Arriving at Port of .... **NEW YORK** ...., 11 FEB 1922 ...., 19

No. on List.	14	15 Whether having a ticket to such final destination.	16 By whom was passage paid?	17 Whether in possession of $50, and if less, how much	18 Whether ever before in the United States; and if so, when and where?			19 Whether going to join a relative or friend; and if so, what relative or friend, and his name and complete address.	20 Purpose of coming to United States.		21	22	23	24	25	26	27 Condition of health, mental and physical.	28 Deformed or crippled, Nature, length of time, and cause.	29 Height.		30 Color of—		31
					If yes— Yes or No.	Year or period of years.	Where?			Length of time alien intends to remain in United States	Whether a polygamist.	Whether an anarchist.							Feet.	Inches.	Complexion.	Hair. Eyes.	Mar
1	Yes	Self	$25	No	-	-	-	Father:- Mr.M.Weiss, 550 Robinson Street,Pittsburgh,Pa.	No	Always	Yes	No	NoNo	No	No No	Good	No	4	8	Dark Blk. Grey	
2	Yes	Self	$25	No	-	-	-	Father:- Mr.M.Weiss, 550 Robinson Street,Pittsburgh,Pa.	No	Always	Yes	No	NoNo	No	No No	Good	No	4	6	Dark Black Grey	
3	Yes	Self	$25	No	-	-	-	Father:- Mr.M.Weiss, 550 Robinson Street,Pittsburgh,Pa.	No	Always	Yes	No	No No	No	No No	Good	No	4	4	Dark Black Grey	
4	Yes	Self	$25	No	-	-	-	Father:- Mr.M.Weiss, 550 Robinson Street,Pittsburgh,Pa.	No	Always	Yes	No	No No	No	No No	Good	No	4	-	Dark Black Grey	
5	Yes	Self	$80		-	-	-	Children 151 Bay 26th Street,Brooklyn,N.Y.	No	Always	Yes	No	No No No		No No	Good	No	5	9	Fresh Grey Hazel	
6	Yes	Husband			-	-	-	Children 151 Bay 26th Street,Brooklyn,N.Y.	No	Always	Yes	No	No No	Cer. 12671 D	No No	Good	No	5	7	Fresh Grey Hazel	
7	Yes	Husband	$25	No	-	-	-	Husband:- Mr.David Cohen, 366 S.Second Street,Brooklyn,N.Y.	No	Always	Yes	No	No No	No	No No	Good	No	5	2	Dark Blk Black	
8	Yes	Father	$25	No	-	-	-	Father:- Mr.David Cohen, 366 S.Second Street,Brooklyn,N.Y.	No	Always	Yes	No	No No	No	No No	Good Cured	No	5	-	Dar k Dark Dark	

Figure 17 Listing of Isadore and family on the Orbita manifest

Figure 18 Sam and wife, Esther, with children Jack and Mel

Figure 19 Wedding photograph of Rose and Harry Weiss in 1928

Figure 20 Harry, Rose and children Marian and Mel (Circa 1934)

Figure 21 Morris Weiss

PART 6
SOCIAL AND GEOGRAPHICAL BACKGROUND RELATED TO JEWISH LIFE IN UKRAINE

The District of Kamenets-Podolski and the Town of Minkovitz by Lewis D. Meixler

Kamenets-Podolski

Before immigrating to the United States, Isadore lived in the town of Minkovitz, which was located about 50 miles from Kamenets-Podolski (also known as Kaminits), a major city in the province of Podolia[3]. Podolia is a Ukrainian province that borders on the regions of Galicia and Bessarabia. The fertile soil supports agriculture and livestock. The region's history dates back to ancient times. The Greek historian Herodotus reported the area was inhabited before the 5th century BCE. It was conquered by the Roman Emperor, Adrianus, and later by various barbaric tribes, which the Slavic tribes drove out in the 6th century CE. Kamenets-Podolski traces its origins back to the 14th century. Initially Lithuanian, it came under the rule of Poland in 1569. From 1672 to 1699 it was under Ottoman rule after which it reverted back to Polish rule and eventually passed to Russia in 1795. It remained the capital of the province of Podolia until the Revolution in 1917. The city of Kamenets-Podolski was an important center for trade and communications. Jews were prohibited from settling in the area until 1447, and were only allowed to visit Kamenets-Podolski for no more than 3 days. In 1598, King Sigismund III prohibited the Jews from settling in the city or the suburbs, from trading in the city and again their visits were restricted to three days only. During the Chmeilnicki led Cossack uprising and pogroms (1648 to 1652) many Jews sought refuge within the fortified walls of the city.[4] In 1648 the insurrectionists took the city and it was reported that some 10,000 Jewish families were murdered[5]

---

[3]   http://www.jewishgen.org/Ukraine/Podolia/Podolia_Gubernia.htm

[4]   Encyclopedia Judaicea, Vol. 10, 1972, Keter Publishing House Jerusalem Ltd. Jerusalem, Israel, Page 725.

[5]   The Universal Jewish Encyclopedia, Vol 6, Ktav Publishing House, Inc. 1969 Page 301

Рис. 6. Фортеця в XVI ст. Вигляд з боку міста. Спроба реконструкції.

Figure 22 16th Century drawing of the walled city of Kamenets-Podolski [6]

---

[6]   Kami'ianets Podolskyi:Istoryko-arkitekturnyi Narys, Kyiv: Budivel'nyk 1968

Figure 23 Contemporary photo of the fortified walled city of Kamenets-Podolski[7]

When the city returned to Polish rule in 1699, the Christian opposition to Jewish settlement resumed. In 1737, the city council submitted a request to the Church and state authorities to ban the Jews from the city, claiming that they had no right to settle there and compete with the Christian inhabitants in trade. King Augustus III expelled the Jews from Kamenets-Podolski in 1750, and the town council seized their houses and the synagogue was demolished. The Jews who were expelled from the city of Kamenets-Podolski settled in the surrounding villages and towns and developed extensive trading activity, which led to additional complaints by the citizens. In 1757 Cardinal Dembowski ordered that a public religious disputation be held in Kamenets-Podolski, between the representatives of the Podolian Jewry and Jacob Frank and his supporters. Jacob Frank was the founder of the Frankist cult, which contained elements of Christianity. After the disputation, the Talmud and about 1,000 other sacred Jewish books were publicly burned in the city on the local bishop's orders. Hasidism[8] originated in what is now Belarus and Ukraine in the middle of the 18th century. Hasidism was popularized by Israel Ba'al Shem Tov (popularly known by the acronym, the Besht), a native of the Podolian town of Koop. Hasidism tended to focus on the role of the rebbe as a spiritual conduit to

---

[7]   http://en.wikipedia.org/wiki/File: Kamianets-Podilskyi-1.jpg
[8]   http://en.wikipedia.org/wiki/Hasidic_Judaism

God, and its followers joined worship groups associated with dynasties of Hasidic spiritual leaders. Hasidism swiftly spread throughout the area and developed into a complete way of life in Podolia, particularly among the common Jewish people, in spite of the opposition of the established Mitnagdim (traditional) rabbis. Hasidism was followed by the Haskalah (secular enlightenment) movement in the latter 18th century and then by the Zionist movement of the 19th century. [9]

After Kamenets-Podolski passed to Russian rule, Czar Paul I allowed the Jews to reside in the city in 1797. At that time there were 1,367 Jewish inhabitants registered on the tax assessment books, and 24 Jews belonged to the merchant guilds. Within two years, the Jewish population had grown to 2,617 and there were 29 Jews in the merchant guilds[10]. In 1832 the Christians again petitioned the government to expel the Jews from the city, based on the same arguments as before. The petition was rejected, but a year later the government restricted the rights of the Jews to build shops and new houses, or to acquire homes in Kamenets-Podolski, and allowed them to live in only two suburbs, in order to prevent them from residing in the city itself. The restriction was lifted in 1859. The Jewish community comprised 40% of the total population of 16,211 in 1897. In 1913 there were about 23,000 Jews in the city. There were many pogroms in the city even after the First World War ended as mentioned in Isadore's book. Kamenets-Podolski suffered severely and 52 Jews were killed in the pogroms of 1919. After the establishment of the Soviet regime, many of the wealthier Jews fled the area and the economy of the Jewish population was ruined. By 1929 only 12,774 Jews remained (29.9%) of the total population.

Kamenets-Podolski was a major center of Jewish leadership and one of the leading rabbis of the community was Isaac Ben Hakim Meisels (d. 1832) who was the father of Dob Berush Meisels, (1798-March 17, 1870) Chief Rabbi of Krakow (Cracow) from 1832 and later, Chief Rabbi of Warsaw (from 1856) [11].

During WW II, after the German occupation of 1941, those Jews who had not managed to escape were murdered. They numbered some 10,000 together with another 6,000 who were brought there from the surrounding area. The Jewish population after WW II was not known and there were no longer any synagogues. [12]

---

[9] Kaminits-Podolsk & its environs: a memorial book of the Jewish communities in the cities of Kaminits-Podolsk, Balin, Dunivits, Zamekhov, Zhvanets, Minkovitz, Smotrich, Frampol, Kupin, and Kitaygorod annihilated by the Nazis in 1941. by Avraham Rosen; H Sarig; Y Bernshtain; Bonnie Schooler Sohn; Bergenfield, N.J. : Avotaynu Foundation, 1999 pages 2-4   http://www.worldcat.org/isbn/0966802101

[10] Encyclopedia Judaicea, Vol. 10, 1972

[11] http://en.wikipedia.org/wiki/Dow_Ber_Meisels

[12] http://yad-vashem.org.il/odot_pdf/Microsoft%20Word%20-%206423.pdf

Figure 24 Map of Ukraine [13]

---

[13] Map of Ukraine, Central Intelligence Agency, Federal Depository Princeton University Library, July 26, 1993

MINKOVITZ

The town where Isadore lived was Minkovitz (Minkowice, Myn'kivci, and also Minkovtsy). The town was located southeast of Lvov and Northeast of Kamenets-Podolski among the hills and forests near the district of Ushitsa. There are several towns with the same name. Isadore's town was located at Latitude: 48.8333, Longitude: 27.2833. The map below shows the town in relation to others in the area.

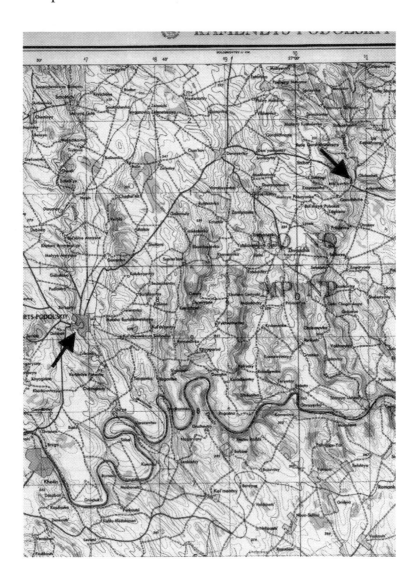

Figure 25 Map showing the location of Minkovitz[14]

Note: The dark line denotes the border with Romania, and the Dnestr River, which Isadore had to cross.

---

[14]   US Army Map 1943, Courtesy of the Princeton University Map Library.

Minkovitz (Myn'kivci) is located about 7 miles West of Novy Ushitsa (Nova Usycja). Note the proximity to Kamenets-Podolsk and the Dnestr River. In the map in Fig. 25, the dark line marks the Romanian border. Minkovitz is at the upper right arrow. Kamenets-Podolsk is at the arrow in the lower left. The dark line is the Dnestr River, which forms the border with Romania. The solid lines are paved roads, and the dotted lines are unpaved. The grid spacing is 10 Kilometers. The contour intervals are 20 meters, which indicates that Minkovitz was located in a deep valley as mentioned by Isadore in his memoir.

A main street ran through the center of town, which led to the Ushitsa River. The Jewish population engaged mainly in commerce and trade, and reached about 5,000 persons prior to WW II. The town had two rabbis and five synagogues, a credit bank, a fire brigade and a committee to visit the sick. [15] Prior to WW I, the Jews in the town lived in about 2,000 dwellings with about 5-6 persons in each, giving it a population of about 10,000 to 12,000. According to tradition, a Jew named Brainin, who was brought from Galicia by a landowner, built the city. The town of Minkovitz consisted of rows of houses, around a central square, where there was a market for cattle, pigs and other commerce. The Jewish community was organized by occupation, such as shopkeepers, merchants, crafts, tailors, cobblers, carpenters, tinsmiths, furriers and artisans. The main trades in the area were agriculture and lumber.

Sundays and Tuesdays were fair days in Minkovitz, and as Isadore mentions in his book, many people came from the surrounding area to buy necessities and sell their produce. The nearest post office was in the town of Novaya Ushitsa, about 12 Km (about 7 miles) East. The Great Synagogue, which was mentioned by Isadore in his book in Chapter 3, "The Night Before the Storm" was built at the time the city was established and was the place where the employers of the workers would come to pray and network. The Holy Ark was adorned with engravings and was noted for its beautifully decorated Ark curtain. The second synagogue was known as the Brick Synagogue, and was where many community affairs were conducted. The third was the Red Synagogue, the fourth Reb Leib's Synagogue and the fifth was Reb Chayiml's Bet Midrash. The Leibovitz family provided many of the town's leaders. There was a bathhouse, a poorhouse, a hostel for the homeless, a burial committee, a shelter for travelers and a cooperative credit bank to help with loans in times of need. As mentioned in Isadore's book in Chapter 12 "The Poles," the town had only one doctor, who was aided by two nurses. The town organized a self-defense unit from among the youth of the town, to defend itself

---

[15] Kaminits-Podolsk & its Environs: a memorial book of the Jewish communities in the cities of Kaminits-Podolsk, Balin, Dunivits, Zamekhov, Zhvanets, Minkovitz, Smotrich, Frampol, Kupin, and Kitaygorod annihilated by the Nazis in 1941 by Avraham Rosen; Ḥ Śarig; Y Bernshtain; Bonnie Schooler Sohn; Bergenfield, N.J. : Avotaynu Foundation, 1999, pages 170 – 171

from pogroms from the Russian soldiers and from Petlura after the end of World War I, as detailed in Chapter 6 "A Pogrom" in Isadore's book. Below is a photo of the Great Synagogue that Isadore mentions in his Chapter 3, from the Yizkor Book created by the survivors of the Holocaust from Minkovitz.

קבוצת יהודי המקום על־יד בית־הכנסת העתיק

Figure 26 "Group of Jews in Front of the [Minkovitz] Old Synagogue" [Hebrew][16]

---

[16] Kamenets-Podolsk u-sevivatah:Sefer zikaron Li-Kehelot Yisra'el Tel Aviv, 1965. Avraham Rosen, Yeshayahu Bernstein and Hayim Sarig. Page 199 [Courtesy Princeton University Library]

Russia 1914-1923   War, Revolution & Pogrom by William "Pat" Schuber

Mother Russia

In October 1939, Winston Churchill, expressing his puzzlement over the recent actions of the Soviet Union in favor of Germany and against Poland uttered this famous statement: "I cannot forecast to you the action of Russia. It is a riddle, wrapped in a mystery, inside an enigma." That statement of frustration could as well been voiced by an American political leader either then or now. Russia has seemed to both attract us and repel us or be the subject of weary fascination over the years, but we ignore this nation at our own peril.

The Russian colossus represents the largest landmass in the world with over 6.5 million square miles extending across Northern Asia and projecting into Europe with 11 time zones stretching over 5,000 miles, from Eastern Europe to the Pacific Ocean. Rich in natural resources including oil and natural gas, Russia has sought to reassert itself in world affairs in most recent times, as it once did, before the fall of communism.

The United States from its earliest times understood the importance of a relationship with Russia. The first U.S. Ambassador was named in December of 1780, but the first Ambassador to take his position in a Russian court in St. Petersburg's was John Quincy Adams in November 1809.

Russia early on became a commercial partner of the United States, with U.S. ships entering Russian ports in the Baltic Sea. Czar Alexander I sought to help mediate an end to the War of 1812, and during the Civil War, Russia gave support to the Lincoln Administration during the nation's most dangerous period.

Despite these early ties, great misunderstandings have separated these two nations, which have been brought about by war, revolution, dictatorship and ideology. Yet a mutual understanding by both nations is now more critical than ever to maintain world peace and stability.

Any attempt to "know" Russia must begin with an understanding of the seminal events, which has shaped the Russian outlook on the world. Such understanding must begin with knowledge of the impact of World War I, the Bolshevik Revolution and the Russian Civil War as the crucibles of fire from which modern Russia has emerged, bloody, battered, but determined.

In the 16th century, Russia, under Ivan IV (The Terrible), was transformed into a multi-ethnic state of rising power and influence. By the beginning of the 18th century under Peter the Great, Russia had "Westernized" and had become a world power. But by the beginning of the 20th century, the Imperial Dynasty, now ruled by Nicolas II, was fraying badly and showing signs of deep and troubling division. Violent, underground organizations (often seen as the predecessor of modern terror organizations) such as the People's Will had emerged and introduced to the world the image of the terrorist as a bomb thrower. A bomb would assassinate Czar Alexander II by this organization.

By 1890-1892, social and economic conflict had broken out across Russia with the resulting death of many. A cholera epidemic during the same time swept away over 2 million people.

The Russo-Japanese War of 1904-1905 had been a disaster for Russia as she was humiliated by the Japanese military on land and on the sea. A revolutionary uprising was initiated in St. Petersburg in 1905 as a result of these wartime depredations. The Czar's grudging institution of a Russian Parliament known as the Duma only tempered such revolutionary violence. The creation of this political stability was an illusion and the uprising of 1905 was an ominous warning of future events.

However, such history of violence and unrest had also ushered in to the world a new and terrible term for brutality against a minority-The Anti-Jewish Pogrom.

THE JEWS AND ANTI-SEMITISM IN RUSSIA

The historical record shows evidence of Jewish settlements in southern Russia, Ukraine, Armenia, and Georgia, as early as the fourth century. In fact, a portion of the ruling classes of Ukraine adopted Judaism as their official religion between the years 650 and 1,000 C. E. [The Khazhari – for example see http://www.khazaria.com/brook.html] By the 11th and 12th century, major Jewish enclaves existed in the Russian principality of Kiev. By the end of the Middle Ages, many Jews had been expelled from Western Europe and had migrated to the more tolerant regions of Central and Eastern Europe. Gradually, many Jews had moved into Poland and thence on to Russia. Middle-sized towns called shtetls were created throughout the region. During these times however, the new Jewish migrants were not assimilated into the existing population, but were identified separately as an ethnic group of its own with a unique set of religious beliefs and occupying a unique economic position.

By the 15th century evidence reveals that small groups of Jews were living in Muscovite, Russia. However, by this time, the Russian sovereign, known as the Tsar, saw himself as the defender of the Russian Orthodox faith. This religious zeal called for strong measures against those perceived to be enemies of the faith, which often included Jews. By the reign of Ivan IV, the Terrible, Anti-Semitism and its brutal treatment of Jews had become imperial policy.

After the Russian partition of Poland in the late 18th century, a large population of Jews had become part of the Russian Empire. Official Russian policy alternated between attempts at assimilation and suppression of independent Jewish life.

The 19th century saw the rise of secret revolutionary movements, which threatened the old, imperial order. As a result, the Tsar's government brutally suppressed many minorities believed to be supportive of these organizations, but particularly the Jews. The first anti-Jewish Pogrom is considered to have occurred in 1821 in Odessa, Ukraine, where anti-Jewish riots resulted in the deaths of several Jews. Other anti-Jewish actions occurred throughout the 19th century. However, the term pogrom became part of the English lexicon after a large-scale anti-Jewish uprising, which swept through southwestern Russia in the early 1880s. These anti-Jewish activities were particularly exacerbated by the assassination of Czar Alexander II for which many blamed the Jews. Thousands of Jewish homes and businesses were destroyed with resulting casualties of killed and injured.

The new Czar, Alexander III, issued harsh new restrictions on the Jews, beginning with the imposition of the so called May Laws, which banned Jews from rural areas, restricted their entry into certain professions, limited entry into universities, and curtailed other freedoms. Waves of pogrom violence continued through 1884, often with the tacit approval, and even the incitement of local government officials and law enforcement. In 1886 The Edict of Expulsion was imposed on Jews in the Kiev region in Ukraine. By 1891, most Jews had been expelled from Moscow. By this time, the Russian Empire had become the home of the largest population of Jews in the world. The 1897 Census of Russia recorded a total Jewish population of over 5 million people, or approximately four percent of the entire population.

As oppression, violence, and deprivation were visited upon the Jews, many chose to become members of the various fledgling revolutionary movements such as The Socialist Revolutionary Party and The Russian Social Democratic Party with both its Bolshevik and Menshevik factions. The concept of overthrowing Tsarist rule was very appealing to Jews as a result of their past treatment by the government. Leon Trotsky, a leading Bolshevik and military leader of the Red Army during the Russian Civil War, is one classic example. From seeking the overthrow of the Tsar, the Bolsheviks promoted a policy of an international, proletarian revolution.

However, anti-Jewish violence continued up to the beginning of the First World War particularly during 1903-1906.

UKRAINE

A nexus of Jewish settlement and Anti-Semitic violence has been Ukraine. The area that we know as Ukraine today in much earlier times was known as the Kievan Rus and was a major center of East Slav power and civilization. It even dominated the entire region at one time, but by the 12th century, its position had disintegrated and by the 14th century, the area had been divided among other regional powers. In the 19th century, Ukraine had been integrated into the Russian Empire, but parts of it were subject to Austro-Hungarian rule. As a result of the chaos of the First World War and the ensuing Russian Civil War, Ukraine would be the scene of horrific violence, death, and depredation. In fact, during 1917-1921, more than 1.5 million Ukrainians would die and anti-Jewish violence would rise to new levels of horror. By 1922, Ukraine would become one of the first founding Republics of the new Soviet Union.

THE COMING OF THE FIRST WORLD WAR

Russia's involvement in the Balkans would bring it into the cataclysm of the First World War. The assassination by a Serbian nationalist of the heir to the Austro-Hungarian throne, the Archduke Franz Ferdinand and his wife Sophie on June 28th, 1914 unleashed a series of tragic events, which ultimately led to the onset of the First World War. An Austrian ultimatum to Serbia, Russia's Slovak ally in the Baltic, caused a Russian military mobilization, which resulted in a declaration of War by Germany, Austria-Hungary's ally.

At the time, the Tsar's army was the largest in Europe, with an initial mobilization of 115 infantry divisions, 38 cavalry, and over 7900 field guns. The Tsar appointed his cousin, the Grand Duke Nicholas, as Commander-in-Chief of all Russian forces. With speed that caught Germans by surprise, Russia was able to penetrate East Prussia, but met a catastrophic defeat at Tannenberg in August 1914. The end of 1914 brought Russian victories that stabilized the front for a period of time. However, by mid-1915, German offensives had expelled Russia from Poland, and one defeat followed another. On August 21, 1915, the Tsar relieved his cousin from command and took over all responsibility for military leadership onto himself. This move did not improve the situation, but only proved to be more disastrous, as the Russians faced further defeats with the Tsar now personally identified with these catastrophic reversals.

One of the enduring images of the coming of the First World War were the joyous crowds waving and cheering in London, Paris, and Berlin as their husbands and sons marched off to war. In fact, one photographer at the time caught the ecstatic face of a young Adolf Hitler in a crowd in Munich hearing the news of Germany's entry into the First World War.

On the surface, the same wave of patriotism seemed to sweep through Russia also. But, throughout Russia, the declaration of war also sparked anti-war riots and unrest, which were quite alarming to the government. In fact, a review of Russian ministry of internal affairs records discloses evidence of violence by military reservists in a number of cities, which resulted in the looting of stores and attacks on policemen.

The façade of stability created by the reforms instituted as a result of the Revolution of 1905 already began to crumble. The incompetence of the government and its military leaders with its accompanying string of defeats and deaths of thousands of soldiers, along with the wide spread shortages of food would shortly bring the entire imperial structure crashing to the ground.

Active opposition to the state's war policy was not limited to soldiers, but rather many civilians took matters into their own hands as the War continued without any end in sight. Workers strikes and periodic violence increased from 1914 into 1915. Desertions from the front accelerated as the Russian army went from defeat to defeat. Revolutionary unrest was found both at the front and at the rear areas. The government attributed these actions to lack of patriotic fervor on the part of the people, but also ominously because of so-called "Jewish" influence in the army, which was believed to be favorable to the Germans. The War in the Western part of the empire had created a wave of millions of refugees fleeing into the Russian interior. Many of these people were either Polish or Ukrainian, countless being of Jewish ancestry. Their movement to the ethnically homogenous Russian settlement was a recipe for trouble.

By 1915, this ethnic cauldron led to wide spread outbreaks of violence. The primary target was the empire's Jewish population. The imposition of martial law had put in charge of public order many with anti-Semitic sentiments. The allegation that was asserted was that the Jewish population was sympathetic to the Germans and even worse, that they were spies and traitors. His Russian officers told the Russian soldier that they were spies, and as a result many were killed. By 1916, ethnic conflict within Russia was widespread. In addition, rising nationalism and the desire for independence by several parts of the empire, particularly Ukraine, were boiling to the surface.

By 1917, demonstrations, strikes, and violent uprisings were becoming an increasingly daily part of Russian life, particularly in the capital, St. Petersburg, now called Petrograd, a less German version of its original name. The failure to impose wartime rationing led to severe shortages of bread in the capital by 1917. On February 1917, workers and their Allies took to the streets demanding food and an end to the war. Military reservists joined them. Other military units refused to fire on the demonstrators and in fact, joined their demonstration. The Tsar shutdown the Duma, but a new quasi-governmental entity had been established known as the Soviet of workers and soldiers. Such Soviets were created in other cities. The Duma refused to close down, and now there were two competing sources of power within the capital, the Soviets representing the workers and soldiers supported by the more radical socialists, and the Duma, attracting the support of the better-educated and commercial elite. The two entities agreed in February to a provisional government and demanded the Tsar's abdication. On March 1, 1917, Nicholas II abdicated his throne, the first of the old empire's had fallen.

THE OCTOBER REVOLUTION

The Provisional Government established by the February uprising opted to continue the war. On April 3, 1917, Vladimir Lenin, leader of the Bolshevik Party and other exiled revolutionaries returned to Petrograd via a sealed train provided by the German army. Upon his arrival, Lenin immediately moved to bring about an end to the Russian participation in the war and preached a slogan of Peace, Land, and Bread. In this simple slogan, he had crystallized the longings of the Russian people. A July attempt by the Bolsheviks to seize power in a coup failed and Alexander Kerensky, a moderate member of the Social Revolutionary Party, emerged as the Prime Minister. One last great offensive was launched against the Germans at his instigation. Known as the Kerensky Offensive, it was a miserable failure, as the attacks ground to a halt and great portions of the front line army melted away.

The commander of the Russian troops, General Lavr Kornilov, in September, accusing the government of collaboration with the Germans, marched on Petrograd. In desperation, Kerensky turned to the Soviets for help. Pro-Bolshevik Red Guards were mobilized and railway workers refused to transport Kornilov's troops. The coup failed. But Kerensky was also a casualty of this incident; he appeared weak and defensive. The Bolshevik's had been galvanized, and accordingly Lenin gave order for the seizure of power.

During the night of October 24-25, 1917, Bolshevik workers, soldiers, and members of the Red Guards, seized government buildings, stormed the Winter Palace, and arrested the provisional government. Kerensky fled, escaping eventually to the West. A government headed by Lenin was proclaimed with the establishment of the Council of Peoples Commissars. Trotsky was put in charge of foreign affairs and a person who would play such a major role in future Russian history, Josef Stalin was named Commissar of Nationalities.

RUSSIA LEAVES THE WAR

Upon seizure of power, Lenin immediately took steps to end Russian participation in the War. Much to the horror of Russia's Western Allies who had visions of millions of German soldiers being transferred from the Eastern Front to the Western Front and potentially tipping the balance in favor of the Germans. A Bolshevik delegation was dispatched to begin negotiations with the Germans. This delegation, eventually headed by Trotsky, after a series of starts, stops, and strategic and tactical delays, signed a peace treaty in March 3, 1918, known as the Treaty of Brest-Latovsk. By this time Germany and her Allies, Austria-Hungary and Turkey had occupied wide swaths of the Western Russian Empire including Poland, the Baltic countries and Ukraine. The Allies in the mean time had attempted to execute a dual-purpose strategy of promising the Bolsheviks recognition and aid if they continued in the war as well as encouraging opposition to the Bolsheviks internally. These policies, which were spearheaded by the British, often worked at cross-purposes to each other, and resulted in the disastrous allied intervention in Russia of 1918.

The new Soviet government wasted no time in consolidating its powers. Opposition, particularly in Petrograd and Moscow, was brutally suppressed. Sweeping measures were introduced to redistribute land, socialize agriculture, create a secret police, "The Cheka", and create a new military organization, The Red Army. In March 1918, the Bolshevik Party renamed itself the Communist Party, and moved the capital from Petrograd to Moscow. In the mean time various nationalists, anarchists, and independent groups sought to establish their control over various parts of the Old Russian Empire. This was especially true in Ukraine, where nationalists, Bolshevik, and anarchist forces fought with each other for control of the region. One of the more infamous anarchists' movements would be the Black Army, led by Nestor Makhno. Some of the most violent actions of the emerging civil war would take place in Ukraine, including the waging of Pogroms against the local Jewish communities.

THE RUSSIAN CIVIL WAR

Little known and studied in the West, the internal violence that emerged in the aftermath of the October Revolution has become known as the Russian Civil

War. Historians of that era still cannot agree on the time frame of this conflict, but it seems to have emerged by the end of 1917 and continued through 1920 with military operations in various places until 1923. For many Westerners, our knowledge of this time period is colored by the romanticized view depicted in the movie Dr. Zhivago, the cinematic adaptation of Boris Pasternak's acclaimed novel. The Russian Civil War would continue the violence and social upheaval that had begun in the Russian Empire at the beginning of the 20th century and had been fatally exacerbated by the First World War. Before it ended over seven million more people would die.

The Russian Civil War was a direct result of the reaction by various elements of Russian society to the seizure of power by the Bolsheviks in October 1917 and their subsequent consolidation of power. Initial counter revolutionary violence broke out in both Petrograd and Moscow shortly after the takeover, but was brutally suppressed. However, the Bolshevik signing of the one sided Treaty of Brest-Litovsk, Bolshevik land policies, particularly the socialization of agricultural land and the suppression of the newly elected Constituent Assembly led to widespread uprisings and opposition throughout the Old Empire. A variety of opponents consisting of Republicans, Monarchists, Nationalists, and more moderate Socialists became collectively known as The Whites. The collective name of this opposition belies the fact that they represented a plethora of interests that had no unity of organization, policy, or principal. Their fatal weakness was their failure of unity of any kind despite several attempts, against a determined enemy, the Communists, now known as the Reds. By early 1918, one of the first military uprisings was led by the Don Cossacks, who resorted to arms against the government and supported several of the White generals, such as general Kornilov. Early on, the Bolsheviks had established control of North Western and Central Russia, which represented the crucial core of Soviet territory industrially and agriculturally. By the beginning of 1918 vast regions representing a majority of the empire's provinces and regions from Poland to the Pacific were in the hands of opposition forces. This included the vitally significant region of Ukraine. One of the key advantages that the Red Forces would have throughout the war is that they, unlike their opponents, would have a hardcore of dedicated, experienced and radical activists hardened by Tsarist oppression and completely opposed to any element of the Old Regime. In addition, Lenin emerged as the most significant and best-organized leader of any element of Russian society. Trotsky, despite his faults, emerged as a significant military leader of the Red Forces if for no other reason that his ubiquitous appearance on all fronts and his easy resort to violent oppression always tended to steel Red opposition at crucial times. In addition, Trotsky was instrumental in the transformation of the new Red Army starting in June 1918. The old Tsarist Army was disbanded (much of it had melted away) and a new army consisting of radical workers and soldier was begun. Eventually, this proved inadequate, and by mid-1918, the Reds had resorted to a forced draft of much of the peasant population. In addition, former Tsarist officers, who had initially been shunned, had been brought back in to service and provided a decisive difference.

From the very beginning, the various White Army military forces were unable to coordinate their various campaigns, and as the Reds continued to control the vital core of the country, they were able to shift their forces from front to front, using interior lines by rail to meet ongoing military emergencies. The Reds faced a number of significant challenges during this War. First, there were the nationalists' uprisings, like that led by the Don Cossacks as well as the Polish War of 1920. Second, there were the complications of the allied interventions in various parts of Russia during 1918-1919. Third, there were the military campaigns of the various White generals such as General A.I. Denikin, General N.N. Iudenich and Admiral A.V. Kolchak. Finally, the most dangerous threat of all was the wide occupation of key Russian territory by German forces as a result of the Treaty of Brest-Litovsk. In the end, the Communists would survive and emerge victorious over all of these obstacles as they turned out to be the most ruthless, well organized and united, in opposition to significantly dysfunctional opponents who never achieved any meaningful public support.

Ukraine represents a microcosm in the extreme violence and turbulence that engulfed the nation. Ukraine represented the largest non-Russian minority within Russia with over 32 million people. Its rich agricultural lands and raw materials made its control absolutely essential to the new government. Initially by the end of the First World War, it had been controlled by a central council known as the Rada, situated in Kiev. But in January 1918, Red forces under Lieutenant Colonel Muraviev captured Kiev and the Rada fled. But German forces occupying Ukraine as a result of the Treaty of Brest-Litosvk had cleared out the Bolsheviks by the spring of 1918 and established a new government under the command of General Pavel Skoropadsky. The Germans and their Austrian Allies represented the biggest threat to the Bolshevik government. The vastness of their military forces, if turned against the government, would certainly have ended the Bolshevik Revolution. It appears that the Germans awoke to the dangers of the Revolutionary ideology that the Bolsheviks represented and began to aid some of the early White Russian forces, but this effort abruptly ended with the collapse of the German Army on the Western front and the November 1918 Armistice which saw the end of the First World War.

As the Germans and Austrians withdrew from Ukraine, the Bolsheviks overthrew the Skoropadsky government in the winter of 1918-1919. The next two years, from 1920-1921, Ukraine became a battle ground between Red forces, the White forces of General Denikin and various nationalists and irregular forces. The Whites perpetrated pogroms against the Jewish population; in particular, Symon Petlura would commit some of the worst depredations. As it was widely believed that the Jewish population favored the Reds, the various White forces sought their suppression in violent pogroms. It is estimated that over 50,000 Jews lost their lives in these actions. In addition, many other members of the Jewish population fled to Poland. By the end of the War, the Bolsheviks had emerged victorious and Ukraine would become one of the founding Republics of the Soviet Union established in December 1922.

ALLIED INTERVENTION

As we have seen, the emergence of the anti-war Bolsheviks had posed a serious threat to the allied position of the First World War. Russia had been a key Western ally and had kept millions of Central Power forces occupied on the Eastern Front. The emergence of the new anti-war government headed by Lenin posed a serious dilemma now for allied War planners. Initial attempts were made to encourage the Russian war effort, but at the same time efforts were made to support potential anti-Bolshevik leaders and forces.

This dual policy would lead to allied intervention in Russia in 1918. One of the earliest backers for intervention was Winston Churchill. Allied forces would land in the Port of Murmansk in the early summer of 1918 and Archangel in August of 1918. Initially the purpose was to protect caches of western arms in those locations, but as relations between the Allies and Bolsheviks deteriorated, elements of the Allied forces came into conflict with Red Forces in the area. The Allies began to give military aid to various White opposition forces. One of these White leaders who benefited from the support was Admiral Kolchak who had seized control of the anti-Bolshevik government in Siberia. However, this government like many other White attempts of administrative control would fail as a result of a lack of popular support and a failure of cooperation between White military leaders and anti-Bolshevik socialists. Other allied interventions took place in the Pacific at Vladivostok where Japanese and American troops would be landed, and in the south where French troops would occupy Odessa and British troops, Baku. But in the end, internal divisions within the Allies and mutual suspicions particularly of Japanese occupation in the far Eastern portion of Russia and the failure of success of White military forces led to the gradual departure of all Allied forces by 1919.

CZECH LEGION

Of all the incidents of the Russian Civil War, one of the most bizarre and yet potentially threatening was the saga of the Czechoslovak Legion. The Czechoslovak Legion was made up of Czechs and Slovaks who had been working in Russia in

1914 when the war broke out. Their homeland was part of the Austro-Hungarian Empire. They decided to fight with the Russians as a unit and by the end of the war this force had grown with the addition of a number of Czech and Slovak POWS captured from the Austro-Hungarian Army. By the end of the War, this unit had grown to two divisions of approximately 40,000 men. The Russian Revolution was not their fight and they sought to aid the Allies on the Western Front in the defeat of the Central Powers and the potential creation of a new Czechoslovak homeland. The only way this could be achieved would be by going east to Vladivostok where they hoped to catch ships that would take them home. In March 1918, the new Soviet government, agreed to allow the Legion to travel by way of the Trans-Siberian Railway from the Volga to the Pacific. But along the way, the members of the Legion came into conflict with a Soviet military force in Urals in May 1918. Moscow overreacted and sought to disarm the Legion and the Czech Legion mutinied. The Legion would now become a focal point for anti-Bolshevik forces in the region. As a result this brought American intervention into Russia to aid the stranded Czechs. The last of the Czechs and the Americans who came to their aid would depart Russia in April and November 1920 as the Reds emerged victorious over their White opponents.

THE END OF THE CIVIL WAR

As White military activity intensified in the various regions of Russia, a failed assassination attempt was made on Lenin's life. This would lead to the implementation by the Bolsheviks of a policy known as the Red Terror. Thousands would be arrested and shot and in July 1918, Lenin would give the order for the execution of the Tsar and his family, then in captivity. This would be a signal to all that there would be no turning back. Thus the Civil War became a cruel and vicious conflict in which terror utilized by one side would be met by terror perpetrated by the other. In the end, White and Red Terror would result in the death of millions of innocent civilians, as the destruction of thousands of villages with resulting famine and disease sweeping vast areas.

In addition, the Communists had imposed what was known as War Communism. War Communism represented the complete mobilization of all elements of the Russian economy to bring about victory in the conflict. This resulted in the nationalization of banks and industry and the socialization of agriculture. By the end of 1920, despite several setbacks, the Reds had emerged victorious over all of their White opponents. Most of the opposition generals and leaders were either dead or had fled.

The final episode in this tragedy would be the Polish campaign of April-October 1920. Just as the Civil War appeared to be over by the spring of 1920, the Army of the newly emerged Poland invaded the Western Plains of Ukraine seeking to take back areas it believed to belong to its country. This led to violent military conflict with the Communists, which resulted in the defeat of the Communist forces led by General Tukhachevsky and Josef Stalin at the very entrance to Warsaw. The Peace of Riga terminated this war in March 1921.

CONCLUSION

While the Russian Civil War had come to an end by November 1920, scattered violence would continue up until 1923. On December 29, 1922, the Soviet Union would be officially established. The Bolshevik Revolution had been consolidated, but much of Russia lay in ruin. Over 7 million people had been killed, and vast areas of the country were subject to disease and famine. The rise of Josef Stalin loomed in the background, Lenin was ailing and new horrors of collectivization, terror, and World War II waited, but then again that is a story for another time.

BIBLIOGRAPHY

Adams, A. E. Bolsheviks in the Ukraine: the Second Campaign, 1918-1919 (Yale University Press, 1963)

Benvenuti, F. The Bolsheviks and the Red Army, 1918-22(Cambridge University Press 1988)

Brovkin, Vladmir. Behind the Front Lines of the Civil War, (Princeton University Press, 1994)

Kenez, P. Civil War in South Russia, 1919-1920: the Defeat of the Whites (University of California Press, 1977)

Mawdsley, Evan. The Russian Civil War. New York: Pegasus Books, 2005.

Radkey, O.H. The Unknown Civil War in Soviet Russia (Stanford University Press, 1976)

Sanborn, Josh. "Riots Before Revolution." Relevance Winter 2002: 9-13.

Steinberg, John. "Russia Leaves the War." Relevance Winter 2002: 14-20.

Swain, Geoffrey. Russia's Civil War. Charleston: Tempus, 2000.

Swain, Geoffrey. Origins of the Civil War (Longman, Harlow 1996)

THE PERSECUTION OF JEWS IN UKRAINE
BY TODD LIEBESFELD, ESQ.

Throughout history, varying regimes has persecuted the Jewish people. As a result of being persecuted, Jewish people were continually forced from their homes in search of new domiciles. In the 8th century, groups of Jewish people established settlements in Ukraine. In the centuries to follow, the Jews established themselves and attained prominence in Ukraine. Culturally, religiously and economically, the Jews had become prosperous. In fact, by the 16th century, Ukraine had one of the largest Jewish populations in the world. However, unfortunately, the semblance of stability was merely an illusion. Specifically, despite a seemingly civil existence in Ukraine, the tentacles of anti-Semitic sentiment that pervaded other parts of the world were also omnipresent in Ukraine. This fact became evident in the mid 17th century when the first recorded acts of genocide in Ukraine against the Jewish population occurred. These acts were just the beginning of a series of orchestrations of persecution and murder to follow over the next two centuries. These ethnically targeted acts are known as pogroms.

A pogrom is a form of riot directed against a particular group, whether ethnic, religious, or other, and characterized by the killing and destruction of their homes, businesses, and religious centers. The term in English is often used to denote extensive violence against Jews — either spontaneous or premeditated — but it has also been applied to similar incidents against other minority groups.

Unfortunately, Jews have been frequent subjects of pogroms dating back to before the existence of the Roman calendar. The first historically reported pogrom against Jews was in 167 B.C.E. when Hellenism was at its peak and Alexander the Great was the leader of the Greeks. The next pogroms against the Jews occurred in Alexandria under Roman rule in 38 A.D. during the reign of Caligula. This anti-Semitic sentiment and aggression persevered for a number of centuries as the Roman Empire continued to have domain over Palestine. (Christians were initially seen as a Jewish sect and were also persecuted during this time period up until the Edict of Milan.) The next pogroms against the Jews occurred in Spain in 1011 and then 1096, both of which were at the hands of the Muslim controlled Spain. The once flourishing Jews in Spain had fallen victim to the Muslim mobs during two significant violent attacks over the 11th century, the former resulting in the death of about 6,000 Jews and the latter resulting in the death of about 4,000 Jews. Then during the Crusades (in the late 11th through mid 12th century), in France, Germany and England, there were a series of pogroms that manifested themselves in violence and genocide. In 1348, during the hysteria attached to the Black Plague, a number of Jews were massacred in Germany forcing many of them to flee to then amiable Poland. The Jews had lived in Poland without fanfare until the Cossacks gained power in the 17th century. This change in dynamics resulted in pogroms against the Jews as well as the Poles. Following these pogroms many Jews fled to Russia and Ukraine.[17] It is in Russia and Ukraine where the worst pogroms in history occurred up until the Holocaust when about 6,000,000 Jews were massacred.

The tension in the Russian and Ukrainian territories had been mounting slowly from the 17th century through the 20th century. As the tension rose over the centuries, so did the acts of violence against Jews. To elaborate, during this vast time frame, these countries struggled with identity issues, civil unrest, assassinations, invasions, industrialization and eventually World War I. This volatility created a number of periods of paranoia and blame. As had been the case in earlier centuries and other parts of the world, the Jews once again became the oft chosen scapegoats for the negative events that plagued these countries. This history, starting with 17th century and peaking during the Russian Revolution is explained in greater detail heretofore.

In 1648-1654, Bogdan Khmelnitsky, a leader of Ukrainian Cossacks, led an uprising against the Polish-Lithuanian Commonwealth magnates with the goal of creating an independent Ukrainian state. As part of his scheme, Khmelnitsky incited the Cossacks[18] to revolt by telling them that the Poles had sold them as slaves to the Jews. Based on the same, the Cossacks killed a large number of Jews, as well as other people believed to be their oppressors. Though the precise number of Jews killed is uncertain, it is estimated to be somewhere in the range 15,000 to 30,000 whereby 300 Jewish communities were destroyed. (It is estimated that, prior to this uprising, the Jewish population in Ukraine was 51,325.)[19]

---

[17]   Please note that from the 17th century to the 20th century, the defining country lines of Russia, Ukraine and other surrounding areas were constantly changing, ambiguous and arguable. Accordingly, the territories that are referred to as "Russia" and "Ukraine" are open to interpretation.

[18]   Cossack people were of mixed ethnic origins, descending from Turks, Tatars, Russians, Ukrainians and others who settled or passed through the vast Steppe that stretches from Asia to southern Europe. (See Cossacks in the German Army, 1941-1945 by Samuel J Newland (1991).

[19]   A History of Ukraine, By Paul Magocsi (1996).

In 1821, following the death of the Greek Orthodox patriarch in Constantinople, the Jews were blamed and anti-Jewish riots in Odessa ensued resulting in the deaths of 14 Jews.

In 1881, the anti-Jewish sentiment in Ukraine, which at the time was part of Imperial Russia, became rampant. From 1881-1917, a large-scale wave of anti-Jewish riots swept through southwestern Imperial Russia. Retrospectively, a large driving force in this mass persecution was the assassination of Tsar Alexander II in 1881. Though the assassination involved a large-scale conspiracy with only one of the conspirators being Jewish, the event was painted as a Jewish orchestrated event. Consequently, the seeds of hatred against Jews were once again planted with the aid of Tsar Alexander III, the son of Alexander II.

Alexander III, who ruled from 1881 – 1884, blamed the Jews for the assassination of his father. Accordingly, from the outset of his reign, he had anti-Semitic policies in place, the most notable of which were the "May Laws," which he instituted in 1882. These policies included creating restrictions on where Jews could live and the occupations that Jews could hold. More significantly, these anti-Semitic policies gave rise to a series of pogroms that continued through his death in 1894 at which time he had just signed orders to have Jews expelled, orders that were carried out immediately upon his death by the new Tsar Nicholas II, Alexander III's son.

It was under Nicholas II, that Ukraine and the rest of the Russian Empire fell prey to civil war, World War I and more pogroms. Nicholas II Alexandrovich Romanov (born on May 18, 1868) was the last Emperor of Russia. His reign was marked by the fall of Imperial Russia from a world superpower to a dilapidated and distraught country. Nicholas II ruled from 1894 until 1917 when he was forced to abdicate the throne as a result of the Russian Revolution.

In 1917, there were a series of popular revolutions in Russia that both affected and afflicted both the Russian State as well as the countries that were controlled by the Russian Empire including Ukraine. These revolutions were ultimately responsible for the displacement of the tsarist autocracy in favor of the Soviet Union. This series of revolutions were later collectively referred to as the Russian Revolution of 1917. The chain of events that made up this revolution is better explained below.

At the beginning of 1917, Russia was ripe for revolution. The country was growing rapidly, giving rise to a diverse group of middle class white collar employees and the evolution of the nobles into new and differing classes such as the proletariats and the capitalists. Meanwhile, there were a significant number of villagers who were impoverished and were forced to migrate from industry to industry as well as place to place just to survive. Accordingly, previously defined social groups were now diluted and fractionalized on every level. Complicating matters further was the emergence of commercialism, a movement that altered the aspirations of many Russian citizens.

As a result of the culmination of all these events, taken together with the lack of efficacy of the government, the concept of revolution began to fester. Specifically, aside from the composite of inequity, varying philosophy and greed, there was a growing resentment for the autocratic state especially in consideration of the rampancy of corruption and antiquated governance. As such, many citizens perceived Tsar Nicholas II as a disinterested leader who was responsible for their oppression. Bolstering these beliefs was the prevalence of inflation and food shortages, as well as the failure to equip the military sufficiently enough to protect the country during World War I. Ultimately, these factors, coupled with prior quasi-revolutionary events led to the Russian Revolution.

The first revolution that occurred in 1917 began in March (although it is referred to as the "February Revolution") in St. Petersburg. Amidst this popular revolution, two factions moved to seize control of the country. The Duma[20] made the first move by capitalizing on the revolution to form the Russian Provisional Government. The Soviets (the workers' council), a more radical socialist faction of Russia, made the second move by agreeing to the Duma's new government with the provision that the Soviets had a say in the control of the government and the militia. Retrospectively, during this revolution, the Russian army was immersed in World War I and did not have further resources to address the insurgency. As such, the army posed no opposition to the revolution and the Tsar, Nicholas II of Russia, relinquished his throne.

The newly formed two-headed Russian State was rife with instability from its inception. The moderate Duma run government and the leftist Soviets continually clashed over their differences. These clashes manifested themselves in frequent mutinies and strikes. Complicating matters further, two more socialist factions entered the civil fray, the Bolsheviks[21] (who formed the Red Guards, a group that was later called the Red Army and is commonly referred to as the Reds) and the Mensheviks.[22]

Said clashes culminated in the next revolution that occurred in November 1917 (the October Revolution). Specifically, the Bolsheviks, who were led by Vladimir Lenin, and the Soviets, overthrew the Provisional Government. After overthrowing

---

[20] The State Duma in the Russian Empire and Russian Federation corresponds to the lower house of the parliament. It is a form of Russian Government, that was formed after the last Czar, Nicholas II. It is also the term for a council to early Russian rulers (Boyar Duma), as well as for city councils in Imperial Russia (Municipal Dumas), and city and regional legislative bodies in the Russian Federation.

[21] The Bolsheviks were Marxist Revolutionaries.

[22] The Mensheviks were sympathizers to the Marxists Revolutionaries.

the Duma, the Bolsheviks appointed themselves as leaders of various government ministries and seized control of the countryside. In order to maintain their rule, the Bolsheviks established the Cheka, a special group dedicated to the ruthless suppression of opponents. Following its seizure of control of Russia, the Bolshevik leadership signed a peace treaty with Germany in March 1918.

With the execution of the peace treaty with Germany, civil war again erupted, though this time between the Red and White (nationalist) factions. This latest war continued for several years, until the Bolsheviks ultimately emerged victorious. In this way the Revolution paved the way for the formation of the Union of Soviet Socialist Republics (USSR). Leading this Revolution was Vladimir Lenin.

Vladimir Ilyich Lenin (born Vladimir Ilyich Ulyanov on April 22, 1870) was born into a successful, educated family of mixed ethnicity. Unfortunately, Lenin's life was turned upside down as a teenager. Specifically, in 1887, when Lenin was 17, his father died from a cerebral hemorrhage. Just over a year later, his oldest brother, Alexander, was arrested and hung for participating in a terrorist bomb plot against Tsar Alexander III.[23] Meanwhile, Lenin's sister, who was with Alexander when he was arrested, was banished. These events radicalized Lenin and apparently led him on a revolutionary track.

This revolutionary track was first born while attending Kazan State University. While there, he gained significant interest in Marxism. This interest began the evolution of Lenin as he found himself embroiled in student Marxist protests. These protests and political expressions eventually resulted in his being arrested and later expelled from the university. Lenin was later permitted to return to college though his new school was the University of St. Petersburg. By 1891 he became a member of the Bar and in 1892 he was awarded a law degree by the university. Though Lenin initially used his license to practice law, he could not escape his pervading interest in promoting Marxist revolutionary propaganda. On December 7, 1895, Lenin was arrested and detained by authorities for about 14 months. Upon his release he was exiled to Siberia where he continued his involvement with local Marxists. This exile paved the way to Lenin's assumption of a significant leadership role in the development of the USSR.

Lenin's first leadership role was as an active member of the Russian Social Democratic Labor Party (RSDLP). Specifically, in 1903, he became the leader of the Bolshevik faction of the RSDLP after it decided to split with the Mensheviks, a split that was largely due to Lenin's revolutionary ideals that became embraced by the Bolsheviks.[24]

---

[23] Christopher Read (2005) Lenin. Abingdon: Routledge.

[24] The Bolsheviks were the majority members of the RSDLP while the Mensheviks were the minority. The reason for the split was that it was decided that party membership should be limited to revolutionary professionals, something the Mensheviks were not.

In November 1905, Lenin returned from Siberian exile to Russia to support the 1905 Russian Revolution where he was soon thereafter elected to the Presidium of the RSDLP. However, when the Revolution was thwarted, Lenin returned to exile though this time to eastern and central Europe. It was not until the Russian Revolution of 1917 that Lenin returned. It was then that Lenin began his true rise to power.

In 1917, World War I was at Russia's doorstep and the Russian Revolution was in its full glory. Nicholas II was forced to abdicate his throne, as his forces were ill equipped to sustain his leadership while fighting against World War I forces and the Revolution at the same time. Upon his abdication of the throne, the new Provisional government was formed. As a proponent of a Marxist type of government, Lenin wanted to ensure that the Provisional government did not thwart the Marxist ideal that his Bolshevik Party had been striving for. Accordingly, Lenin wanted to take this opportunity to empower the Bolsheviks. However, it was initially difficult for him to travel through Europe to Russia as World War I was raging everywhere. Nevertheless, Germany decided to grant Lenin safe passage to Russia as it was their hope that Lenin's presence would further destabilize Russia and give Germany less concern about Russia's war efforts.

Upon his arrival in April 1917, Lenin immediately took a leading role in the Bolshevik movement in an effort to promote uncompromising opposition to the newly formed provisional government. While the Bolsheviks had grown stronger and had some great leaders such as Leon Trotsky, Lenin realized that the Party had still not garnered enough support to overtake the newly formed government. This fact was evident when a non-Bolshevik led revolt occurred in July against the new government's troops, a revolt that was stifled easily. In order to avoid being arrested for the revolt that was blamed on the Bolsheviks regardless of their lack of direct role, Lenin once again fled the country. Though out of the country, he published writings to encourage the workers to push for a government run by worker's councils, which were also known as Soviets. Within a couple of months, the Bolshevik Party had gained the support of enough of the laborers to engage the Provisional government. As such, Lenin returned in October to lead a Bolshevik revolt against the Provisional government. By November 8, 1917, the Provisional government was ousted and Soviet rule had begun.

On November 8, 1917, the Russian Congress of Soviets elected Lenin the Chairman of the Council of People's Commissars. From the outset of his leadership, he made it clear that it was important to him that the country be uniformly modernized and cultured so as to ensure that the suffering of the Russian people would be a thing of the past. To that end he promoted the expansive use of electrical lines and means of travel throughout the country. He also initiated an economic recovery plan that would create universal health care for all, while also working on issues of literacy and the rights of women. However, on the forefront was the continuation of World War I. It was Lenin's desire to avoid any further damage to Russia by signing a peace treaty with Germany. However, other Bolshevik leaders were hesitant to sign any treaty without certain preconditions. As Germany would not agree to a conditional treaty, Germany renewed its war efforts, causing Russia to lose much of its western territory; consequently Lenin's original peace treaty ideas became embraced by the Bolsheviks. As such, on March 3, 1918, a peace treaty was reached whereby Russia lost significant territories in Europe.

On two different occasions in 1918, assassination attempts were made on Lenin. In 1921, as a result of these assassination attempts, Joseph Stalin, a trusted confidant of Lenin argued for a policy of "open and systematic mass terror" to be instigated against "those responsible." The other Bolsheviks agreed, and instructed Felix Dzerzhinsky, whom Lenin had appointed to head the Cheka in 1917, to commence a "Red Terror", which was officially announced to the public on September 1, 1918, by the Bolshevik newspaper, Krasnaya Gazeta.[25]

As instructed the Cheka perpetrated mass executions of groups seen as opponents of the Bolshevik regime. [These anti-Bolsheviks (anti-Reds) were referred to as Whites.] It is estimated that about 280,000 people (believed to be Whites by the Reds) were executed from 1918-1920 -- some people for taking part in rebellions, some for membership of counter-revolutionary organizations, some for gangsterism, some for incitement to revolution, some for corruption, and the rest for desertion and espionage.[26] Additionally, it is estimated that by September 1921 there were more than 70,000 people put in labor camps.[27]

While the Reds had committed numerous atrocities, so did the Whites. In fact, according to historian Christopher Read the numbers killed by the White forces were on a comparable scale to the Bolsheviks and can probably be numbered in hundreds of thousands. For instance, the Whites killed 115,000 Ukrainian Jews in 1919 alone.[28] While the facts and scope of the acts of Reds and Whites during this time period are disputable, the reality is that once again the Jews became a victimized group.

In view of the above, what is clear is that from Alexander III's reign in 1881 through the Bolshevik rule in the 1920's, a once flourishing Ukrainian Jewish population was decimated. During each regime of that period, one faction or another singled out the Jewish population for persecution and genocide. Accordingly, when reading the manifest of this book, it is important to understand that the author of

---

[25] The Rise of Stalin: AD1921–1924. History of Russia. History World. Retrieved on 2008-07-19.

[26] Robert Lewis; ed. Mark Harrison, RW Davies, S.G Wheatcroft (1994). The Economic Transformation of the Soviet Union. Cambridge University Press. pp. 188.

[27] Péter Szegedi Cold War and Interpretations in Quantum Mechanics.

[28] Christopher Read (2005) Lenin: A Revolutionary Life: 250.

the manifest lived through a time of almost persistent fear and horror. Specifically, this time frame was associated with the most horrific spectacle of mass genocide against the Jews in history up until the Holocaust. It is estimated that during this period, 70,000 to 250,000 Jews were killed.

POGROM, THE RUSSIAN WORD FOR RIOT
BY JOEL LIEBESFELD

In the last decades of the Czarist rule, attacks against the Russian Jewish population became commonplace. The Jews, as victims were given no sympathy from the Russian rulers or from the majority of the surrounding population. The apathy about the Jewish problem ran across the entire spectrum of Russians. The educated, uneducated, the ruling class gave no form to the terrorism which was upgraded to looting, rape and murder. The Jewish response appeared to crescendo by 1881. The Jews began to rebel against the czar in ways that would have been unheard of in previous times. Desperation was the impetus for the Jews to revolt against the czars and seek their ouster and join movements for the overthrow of the rulers. Jews became very nationalistic although many turned to mass migration.

Many survivors of that Russian era came to this country in poor health as a result of being malnourished from living in poverty or from performing backbreaking work in unhealthy conditions or from taking beatings from Russian soldiers/gangsters or from the depression of seeing their wives and daughters raped and abused. Little or no medical help was available in Russia or Eastern Europe to the Jews who lived in the era of the pogroms.

Anti-Semitism is a hatred of the Jews. The Germans and the Russians throughout the last decades of the 19th century legitimized a new type of hatred of Jews. Formerly, hatred for the Jews was based upon a perception of the alienation of these religious followers from the larger major religious groups. The evolved anti-Semitism of the late 19th century expressed hatred for alleged economic and social anomalies credited to the Jews. The end game was that the Russians thought so little of its Jewish population that they invented the pogroms as a means of demonstrating to the non-Russian population, a way to deal with the misery that was overtaking that part of the world.

The mindset of the expendability of Jews is at the heart of ant-Semitism in all of its forms. The Russians invented excuses to punish and exploit the Jews, as did the Aryan culture. One reason that the Germans did not move aggressively against Christianity was that the Germans felt that they could capitalize on Christian zealots that wanted to take revenge against the Jews for what they believed was the cause of the demise of Jesus Christ. The saving grace for Jews in the relationship with most

Christians, especially in modern times, is that, "not only was the Christian God a Jew, but St. Paul, the originator of Christianity, was a Jew." [29]

The Russian actions against the Jews in the late 19th Century helped set the foundation of what was later to become the Aryan "final solution." In Eastern Europe the Germans were going to exterminate the Jews to rid them as a threat. As vicious as the Russian pogroms were, the riotous activities were mainly confined to hooligans working for a narrow political leadership. The German governmental leadership by WWII was in the hands of sociopathic personalities certainly as it regarded the Jewish population. The German level of hatred had risen to a point where the German children were being taught that Jews were not human.

During the period between the late 1880s and the 1920s most of the newly arriving émigrés came to America penniless. Despite the humblest of beginnings, some became towering figures in American history. For example, Arthur Goldberg was born on the West Side of Chicago in 1908. He was the last of 11 children and worked from the time he was 8 years old. He held jobs as a delivery boy, fish wrapper, etc., while attending night school. He graduated from De Paul University and Northwestern Law School. [30]

Arthur Goldberg was the son of Ukrainian Jewish immigrants who rose through poverty to become the Secretary of Labor to President John F. Kennedy and was appointed to the Supreme Court by the same president, and later resigned that job to accept an appointment as the Ambassador to the United Nations for President Lyndon B. Johnson. [31]

There are many famous Jews from Russia, Ukraine, and Belarus. Some of the names are more common than others because many are more known outside of American borders. This is a list that should have some names familiar to most readers; Isaac Levitan (Landscape Artist), Lev Landau (Physicist), Osip Mandelstam (Poet and Essayist), Shalom Aleichem-Rabinowitz (Writer), Boris Pasternak (Nobel Prize Laureate in Literature), Anton Rubinstein (Pianist, Composer and Conductor), Sergei Eisenstein (Film Director), Grigori Perelman (Mathematician), Leon Trotsky (Bolshevik Revolutionary and Marxist Theorist), and Isaac Babel (Journalist, Playwright and Short Story Writer), Babel survived the 1905 pogrom in which his father and 300 others were murdered. Isaac was saved with the help of Christian neighbors. [32]

---

[29] Pasachoff, Naomi, and Littman, Robert J. Jewish History in 100 Nutshells. Jason Aronson Inc., Norvale, New Jersey 1996

[30] Schlesinger, Arthur M. Jr. The Almanac of American History. Connecticut 1993

[31] See http://www.jewishvirtuallibrary.org/source/biography/Agoldberg.html visited on Tuesday, November 11, 2008

[32] See http://en.wikipedia.org/wiki/List_of_Russia_Jews visited on Tuesday, November 11, 2008

YIZKOR BOOKS AS A SOURCE OF
GENEALOGICAL INFORMATION
BY DR. EAMON P. DOHERTY

The survivors of many of the communities of Europe that were destroyed by the Nazis in World War II created Yizkor Books as memorials to those towns and victims who perished in the Holocaust. The Yiddish word "Yizkor" means remembrance. Yizkor books document the regions where the Jewish communities where annihilated by the Nazis. The Yizkor books contain the memories of the communities, the synagogues, the schools, and personal stories that were significant to them. These books serve as a legacy to the lost families and communities.

The Yizkor Book for Isadore's town of Minkovitz, Ukraine is "Kamenets-Podolsk & Environs." The book is a Memorial of the Jewish Communities in the Kamenets-Podolsk region, which were Balin, Dunivits, Zamenkhov, Zhvanets, Minkovitz, Smotrich, Frampol, Kupin, and Kitay Gorod. The Nazis annihilated all in 1941. Abraham Rosen, H. Sarig, and Y. Bernstein edited the book. The Kamenets-Podolsk and other Yizkor books are available from the Jewish Collection of books in the New York City Public Library and other major public and University libraries. Some are available electronically. The Yizkor book is also available in Hebrew. Kamenets-Podolsk u-sevivatah: Seder Zikaron Li-Kehelot Israel Tel Aviv, 1965. Avraham Rosen, Yeshayahu Bernstein and Hayim Sarig.

The Yizkor book for Minkovitz has a section that describes how a Rabbi was in charge of recording the names of who were born, married and who died in the town. The Rabbi had to tend to the sick, visit people, and perform many services in the community. The account goes on to report that if he was extremely busy he sometimes entrusted the duty of writing the names to various less capable family members in a book known as a "Book of the Living."[33] Sometimes the names were purposefully written incorrectly to avoid military service for the Czar. The estimates for the Jewish population of Minkovitz vary according to those interviewed[34] but

---

[33] Kaminits-Podolsk & Its Environs, Yizkor Book On Loan from the NYC Public Library, Published by Avotaynu Foundation Inc., Bergenfield, New Jersey, 1999. Page 175

[34] Kaminits-Podolsk & Its Environs, Page 170

one source said it was about 5,000 people, five synagogues, a fire brigade, two Rabbis, and a credit bank[35]. I assume that number could be higher or lower when Isadore lived there due to births, emigrations, military conscription, and massacres from Petlura or Deniken lead pogroms. It is noteworthy that there exist at least three common spellings for the name Petlura. However, they all refer to the same person known as Symon Petlura. Anti-revolutionary forces, some from outside of Russia, supported him. It is also unfortunate that he, like Josef Stalin, started out as a seminarian.

In the Yizkor book for Minkovitz, Hayyim Druckman wrote a story that describes how a fat pimple faced youth who was with the outlaw Petlura, broke into his house and shook his bed. He said some awful things to him and made him go at gunpoint to a place where Jews were often murdered. The pimple faced youth, as Hayyim described it, made him walk back and forth five or six times. Hayyim and his family begged and pleaded with the youth to spare Hayyim's life. Each time the man threatened to shoot him. After terrorizing him repeatedly for his amusement, he finally let Hayyim go, but said he was coming back for him. The story is consistent with many of the horrors that Isadore discusses.

---

[35]   Kaminits-Podolsk & Its Environs, Page 169

PART 7
THE FORMATION PROCESS OF THIS BOOK
BY DR. EAMON P. DOHERTY

MOTIVATION FOR THE BOOK

This book is a compelling narrative of a very young Isadore Weiss and his mother, brothers, and sister in Ukraine in the early twentieth century. Deb and Lew Meixler remarked that they had taken Isadore to see the movie "Reds" and Isadore stated that the movie seemed to be an accurate portrayal of the events of the Russian Revolution as he recalled it. Isadore describes life in his small town of Minkovitz before experiencing the horrors of World War I. A particularly poignant chapter is his vivid recollection of a frightening night spent alone in the dark empty main synagogue of his town. Then he describes the many hardships such as hunger, bitter cold and lack of work that existed around the time of the October Revolution. He points to the good side of humanity from caring gentiles who risked their lives by providing food and hiding Jewish people from the pogroms. The German military occupiers showed compassion for the town's people by carving toys made from wood for the children and building a trash disposal system for the community. We see the kindness of many Jewish people who tried to share what little food and clothing they had with barefoot starving German prisoners of war who were marched back to Russia. One can also feel the wonder and surprise of Isadore and the villagers as they see their first airplane, car and motorcycle. After the Bolshevik Revolution, life became more hopeful for Isadore and his family as the noble's land was distributed to the peasants for farming. Finally, Isadore's family received money from his father in Pittsburgh, and they move to the United States where he ultimately meets Sylvia, marries, and has children.

THE SCHOLARLY INVESTIGATIVE WORK FOR THIS BOOK

This book needed a certain amount of scholarly investigation. My steps were to read related academic material, followed by an interview with Sylvia Weiss, Isadore's wife, to discuss the memoir and related photos. I also asked for an interview with Sylvia to discuss her life. This was useful to write the prologue and other background that was needed to understand the main events in the memoir. I also arranged to film Sylvia, who is nearly a century old. Her view on this segment of turbulent history is valuable.

COLLECTING THE MATERIAL

You may wonder how I acquired this material for this book. It started by my discussion of my chapter of Uncle Bob's experiences in Nagasaki in my book, "Emergency Management and Telemedicine for Everyone." Lew Meixler, a friend and fellow New Jersey Homeland Security Technology Committee member, told me about his father-in-law's memoir and audiotapes of his experiences in the Russian Revolution. Once I had the lead, I followed it up and got the memoir.

I learned from Lew Meixler, that his father-in-law had written a memoir that was interesting and had historical significance. I made arrangements with his family to copyright the material and make a contract for publishing. The story also discussed historical figures such as Leon Trotsky, which made me feel it should be published.

SCANNING THE PAPER MEMOIR TO AN ELECTRONIC FORMAT

The typed written paper memoir was on old paper. Some of the letters had faded and letters such as an 'e' could easily be mistaken for a 'c.' I must applaud Lew's daughter, Marci, for scanning all 151 pages of the memoir and creating a PDF format document of only 6 megabytes. The PDF could easily be emailed as an attachment for a potential publisher to read. However, I found there were some misspellings that I wished to correct. I also could not use the document in its present form for publishing. I then used an optical character recognition program to change the PDF document to a Microsoft Word Document. Once the conversion was done, then the corrections started. Words such as "had" were sometimes replaced with "bad". There were even some potentially embarrassing mistakes. My mother and I did several iterations of proof reading, with a series of final editing, proof readings and corrections by Deb and Lew Meixler.

INVITING CO-AUTHORS TO CONTRIBUTE

I feel it is important to select people for co-authors who can increase the knowledge the reader can gain from the book. Every co-author has asked for the book signing poster and has had it framed as a keepsake of the book. Allowing others to participate in the selection of the colors and artwork in the book signing also allows for people to work together and do something creative that will be in print for many years. This poster and book together becomes a legacy. My mother and her brother Uncle Bob enjoyed working together on a previous book called, "A New Look at Nagasaki, 1946."

SELECTING A PUBLISHER

It is important to select the correct publisher for your needs. I selected Authorhouse because they allow me to retain the copyright and I can sell the book to a movie company as a script if I wish. I also get the royalties along with easy to read statements about sales. Lastly they obtain for me an ISBN number as well as web space on famous online bookstores such as Amazon and Barnes and Noble. Authorhouse also uses on demand printing, which means they will take care of orders from 1 book to 1 million and nothing extra is printed or wasted. Authorhouse also has very friendly and knowledgeable people on their staff.

THE BOOK SIGNING AND POSTER

It is important to have a book signing so that people who wrote the book and their families can get together with a few readers. It is important to celebrate all the work they put into their book. It is also important to create a poster for a book. Posters should include: the title of the book, a section about the author(s), a graphic of the book, and a synopsis of the book containing 300 words or less.

PART 8 ACKNOWLEDGEMENT BY DR. EAMON P. DOHERTY

Lew Meixler coordinated the collection of all the research materials for the book such as the maps, Kamenetz-Podolski images, the Minkovitz synagogue photo, the Weiss family photos, immigration and ship photos, and the Yizkor Books for Kamenetz-Podolsk, which documents Minkovitz and other Jewish communities in Ukraine. He organized the submission of the material for the book, provided the audiotapes of Isadore and put them into a format compatible for computer listening. He also drove his mother-in-law to the interviews where she discussed the book. He also provided the original memoir and digitized photographs in the correct resolution for the book. He contributed the section "The District of Kamenets-Podolski and the Town of Minkovitz." He is married to Deborah [Deb] Meixler, Isadore and Sylvia's youngest daughter. He and Deb proofread and made corrections and comments through multiple iterations for the book. I should also mention that they did these things freely, and always with a smile. Sylvia and Isadore's other children are Mona Gottesman, Marc Weiss and Miriam Zwerin (deceased). Deb and Lew and their son, Michael and daughter, Marci felt it was important to preserve Isadore Weiss' memoir and to present it with the context of the history of the region where Isadore lived for future generations for the Weiss family and for others who may wish to study Isadore Weiss' recollections. To make the primary material easily available to others, Marci scanned the original typewritten version of "Looking Back" into a PDF to convert it to digital format and their son, Michael Meixler, created and maintains the WEB site [www.isadoreweiss.com] which contains all the photos, the original "Looking Back" manuscript in its original format and the audiotapes that were recorded by Melvin Weiss. Others in the family contributed materials and memories. Lew said we are all grateful for Eamon's enthusiastic encouragement, and they are all proud to be part of establishing this book to preserve Isadore's manuscript as a lasting tribute to Isadore Weiss and his extraordinary prescience in writing "Looking Back."